Daily
INSIGHTS

to

BIRTHING
the
MIRACULOUS

HEIDI BAKER

CHARISMA
HOUSE

Most CHARISMA HOUSE BOOK GROUP products are available at special quantity discounts for bulk purchase for sales promotions, premiums, fundraising, and educational needs. For details, write Charisma House Book Group, 600 Rinehart Road, Lake Mary, Florida 32746, or telephone (407) 333-0600.

DAILY INSIGHTS TO BIRTHING THE MIRACULOUS by Heidi Baker
Published by Charisma House
Charisma Media/Charisma House Book Group
600 Rinehart Road
Lake Mary, Florida 32746
www.charismahouse.com

Cover design by Lisa Rae McClure
Design Director: Justin Evans

Visit the author's website at
http://www.irisglobal.org/.

Library of Congress Cataloging-in-Publication Data:
An application to register this book for cataloging has been submitted to the Library of Congress.
International Standard Book Number: 978-1-62998-914-3
E-book ISBN: 978-1-62998-915-0

Portions of this book were previously published by Charisma House as *Birthing the Miraculous* by Heidi Baker, ISBN 978-1-62136-219-7, copyright © 2014; *Compelled by Love* by Heidi Baker with Shara Pradhan, ISBN 978-1-59979-351-1, copyright © 2008.

First edition

16 17 18 19 20 — 9 8 7 6 5 4 3 2 1
Printed in China

CONTENTS

INTRODUCTION

He has told you, O man, what is good—and what
does the LORD require of you, but to do justice and to
love kindness, and to walk humbly with your God?
—MICAH 6:8

My husband, Rolland, and I live in
Mozambique. We spend some part of each
week visiting backcountry villages. We are
familiar with simple village life in places without power, running water, or large amounts of
contact with the outside world.

The Lord has done miraculous things
in our lives. We have given a lot to be here,
but we fall more in love with Jesus every
day. If we had another thousand lifetimes,
we would give them all away for love's sake.
Every breath, every moment, everything we
have—we would give it all!

As you read these daily devotions, allow
God to open your eyes. Learn to live in the
intimate love of God. Believe that God can

take you who are well fed and well clothed and make you hungry, thirsty, desperate, and completely dependent on your Father's love so that your eyes will see those around you who are in need of fresh bread from heaven. Then trust Him to change their lives by birthing the miraculous through you!

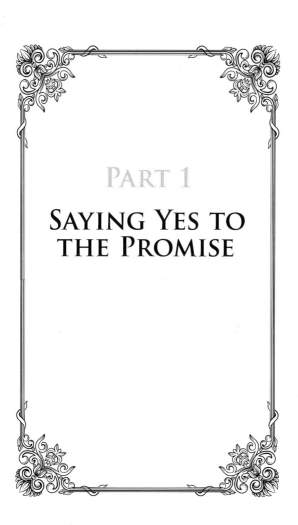

PART 1

SAYING YES TO THE PROMISE

DAY 1
YOU CALL THIS "FAVOR"?

*In the sixth month the angel Gabriel was sent
from God to a city of Galilee named Naza-
reth, to a virgin betrothed to a man whose name
was Joseph, of the house of David. And the virgin's name was Mary. The angel came to her and
said, "Greetings, you who are highly favored. The
Lord is with you. Blessed are you among women."*

*When she saw him, she was troubled by his words,
and considered in her mind what kind of greet-
ing this might be. But the angel said to her, "Do
not be afraid, Mary, for you have found favor with
God. Listen, you will conceive in your womb and
bear a Son and shall call His name JESUS."*

—LUKE 1:26–31

Notice that Mary did not jump up and
down with excitement at the news the angel
brought to her. In fact, she was "troubled
by his words." What young, unmarried girl
wouldn't be troubled if an angel appeared in

her room to tell her she would become pregnant by the favor of God? Because we know how important Jesus's incarnation was for our eternal destiny, we don't often consider how disturbing this news was to Mary. What would she do? How would she tell her parents and her fiancé?

We all think we want a word from God, but would we want to receive one like this? Mary's example teaches us that sometimes the most spectacular miracles will get us into equally spectacular trouble. Her gift had harsh consequences. She could hide it for only so long. Eventually her promise started to show, and she had to give an account for it.

Sometimes God's promises will look like this: bizarre, implausible, and even crazy. At times great promises will invite misunderstanding from those around us—even to the point of reproach.

If we desire the favor of God in our lives, we should consider what it might look like. It is not always going to be cash and promotions and the like. Mary's favor was that of a simple Jewish girl who suddenly found herself pregnant. In all likelihood, she had to deal with terrible gossip, criticism, and disapproval from her community. Yet she had to nurture, protect, and love the life growing within her despite a great deal of misunderstanding and pain.

Thought for Reflection

Considering the difficulty and awkwardness of Mary's situation when God chose her to be the mother of His Son, search your heart: Are you ready to seek God's favor in your life, even though you may be "troubled" when He tells you what that means?

Prayer

Thank You, Lord, for Your favor. Help me to receive it with grace, even when the promises that accompany it don't make sense to me.

DAY 2
WHAT WILL PEOPLE THINK?

Now Israel loved Joseph more than all his sons, because he was the son of his old age, and he made him a coat of many colors. But when his brothers saw that their father loved him more than all his brothers, they hated him and could not speak peaceably to him.

Now Joseph dreamed a dream, and when he told it to his brothers, they hated him even more. He said to them, "Please listen to this dream which I have dreamed. We were binding sheaves in the field. All of a sudden my sheaf rose up and stood upright, and your sheaves stood around it and bowed down to my sheaf."

His brothers said to him, "Will you really reign over us, or will you really have dominion over us?" So they hated him even more because of his dreams and his words.

Then he dreamed another dream and told it to his brothers and said, "I have dreamed

*another dream. The sun and the moon
and eleven stars were bowing to me."*

*But when he told it to his father and his
brothers, his father rebuked him and said
to him, "What is this dream that you have
dreamed? Will I and your mother and your
brothers really come to bow down ourselves to
you to the ground?" So his brothers were jealous
of him, but his father kept the matter in mind.*
—GENESIS 37:3–11

When we receive a promise from God, we're not likely to receive kudos for it. If He speaks to us in an unusual way, gives us a strange task, or tells us to go somewhere unexpected, we may be ostracized. In fact, we may be hesitant to tell our friends and family about it for that very reason. We quite naturally worry about how people will react. Remember Joseph? When he told his brothers about the prophetic dreams he had received from God, they sold him into slavery to try to prevent them from being fulfilled. And what about Noah? When he began building the ark at God's command, people laughed at him.

Imagine for a moment how Mary felt when she had to tell her family about her visitation and about the wonderful promise from God now growing within her—not only that she was a virgin but also that the child within her was the Son of God, Israel's Messiah. Say what? That's a pretty big claim!

Sometimes we wonder how we are going to explain far simpler things to people. Not everyone sees the wisdom in giving everything away before going to sit with the destitute in bombed-out, third-world streets. Not everyone understands forty-day fasts. Not everyone understands going to preach Jesus in places where you could be stoned for doing so. Not everyone understands giving your entire life to care for victims of the sex-trade industry in India. And not everyone understands even less radical calls such as giving up a career to start a home church in your local area.

The truth is that sometimes our family and friends will not understand the destiny we carry. Even if they do, their approval and support may not come until ten or twenty years after we have embraced it.

Thought for Reflection

How important is it to you for other people to approve of your calling and your decision to walk with God to fulfill it? What if your family or those close to you don't support your calling? Will you continue to pursue your destiny?

Prayer

Lord, give me the grace and strength to follow You, no matter how many people criticize me, reject me, or fail to understand why I am doing what You ask me to do.

DAY 3
JUST SAY "YES"

*But the angel said to her, "Do not be afraid, Mary,
for you have found favor with God. Listen, you
will conceive in your womb and bear a Son and
shall call His name JESUS. He will be great, and
will be called the Son of the Highest. And the
Lord God will give Him the throne of His father
David, and He will reign over the house of Jacob
forever. And of His kingdom there will be no end."*

*Then Mary said to the angel, "How can
this be, since I do not know a man?"*

*The angel answered her, "The Holy Spirit will
come upon you, and the power of the Highest will overshadow you. Therefore the Holy
One who will be born will be called the Son
of God. Listen, your cousin Elizabeth has also
conceived a son in her old age. And this is the
sixth month with her who was declared barren. For with God nothing will be impossible."*

Mary said, "I am the servant of the Lord.
May it be unto me according to your word."
Then the angel departed from her.
—LUKE 1:30–38

Mary's question was understandable. "I've never participated in a procreative act, so how can I possibly conceive a child?" It's essentially the same question we ask when God calls us to do something that seems impossible: "How can I do *that?* I don't have the gifts, talents, resources (or whatever else we think we need)." God's answer to us is the same as it was to Mary: "By the power of the Holy Spirit." It's not up to us to make God's promises come to pass; it's up to us to surrender and say yes to whatever He is asking us to do. Then He will provide all that we need.

Many years ago I attended a conference at the Toronto Airport Christian Fellowship (now Catch The Fire Toronto). At the conference Randy Clark preached with great fire and conviction about the anointing, power, and destiny God wants to release upon us. In the middle of his message I suddenly began to feel such desperation for God that I could not hold myself back from responding. There was no altar call—not even a pause in his message—but in front of thousands of people I felt compelled to run up to the altar. I knelt down there, lifted up my hands, and started screaming.

Randy stopped preaching. He put his hands on me and said, "God wants to know, do you want the nation of Mozambique?" Having previously asked God, during a powerful encounter, to give me a nation, I screamed, "Yes!," with everything in me. Randy continued, "The blind will see, the deaf will hear, the crippled will walk, the dead will be raised, and the poor will hear the good news."

I still remember the cry of yes that passed directly from my heart to God's. I didn't think about it. If I had thought about it, I probably would have screamed no. But that would not have been what God wanted. As unlikely a candidate as I was, He wanted to use me to help the entire nation of Mozambique come to know Him.

What is it that God wants from you? What has He promised He would do through you? Whatever it is and no matter how impossible it seems, respond as Mary did, with a yielded cry of yes.

Even the smallest yes matters to God.

Thought for Reflection

What do you think God desires for you to do? Is there anything you would withhold from Him or refuse to do if He asked?

Prayer

Lord, help me to say an enthusiastic, unqualified yes to whatever You ask of Me. Help me to believe that no matter how impossible Your promises seem, You can bring them to pass and use me as a catalyst for Your glory to be manifest on the earth.

DAY 4
THE COST OF SAYING YES

*Now the birth of Jesus Christ happened this way:
After His mother Mary was engaged to Joseph,
before they came together, she was found with child
by the Holy Spirit. Then Joseph her husband, being
a just man and not willing to make her a public
example, had in mind to divorce her privately.*

*But while he thought on these things, the angel
of the Lord appeared to him in a dream saying, "Joseph, son of David, do not be afraid to
take Mary as your wife, for He who is conceived in her is of the Holy Spirit. She will bear
a Son, and you shall call His name JESUS, for
He will save His people from their sins."*

*Now all this occurred to fulfill what the
Lord had spoken through the prophet, saying, "A virgin shall be with child, and will bear
a Son, and they shall call His name Immanu-
el," which is interpreted, "God with us."*

*Then Joseph, being awakened from sleep,
did as the angel of the Lord had commanded him, and remained with his wife.*
—MATTHEW 1:18–24

Have you ever hesitated to say yes to God? If so, it was probably because you know saying yes to His promises can be costly. Mary knew there would be a price to pay when she said yes to His request for her to bear His Son.

Personally I believe she could have said no. She might have said something like, "You are awesome. You are beautiful. But you are scaring me. Please. I am a virgin. I do not want this. Find someone else." She might have been overwhelmed by the prospect of shame, of ridicule, or perhaps of losing her betrothed. In the Lord's manifest presence we may be stirred with profound emotion and receive lofty promises, but what happens afterward?

After I said yes to God at the conference in Toronto, our circumstances became more challenging than ever. My husband, Rolland, came down with severe malaria. I was diagnosed with multiple sclerosis. Our financial situation became even worse. Our Mozambican children were living in tents with worms and with rats biting their toes at night.

Through all this I kept believing in the word given to me through Randy Clark—that God would give me the nation of Mozambique. During that whole year I prayed for healing for all the blind people I met in that country. They all met Jesus, but none of them saw.

Then, after one year, God opened the heavens. The word started coming true. The blind began to see. The deaf began to hear. The crippled began to walk. Three of our Mozambican pastors raised people from the dead. Church growth exploded. Our history ever since has been filled to the brim with wild and wonderful tales.

When the Lord spoke to me about His desire for the entire nation of Mozambique to know Him, it felt bizarre for Him to ask me for help. We had experienced limited ministry success according to the world's standards. We had seen a few miracles, but by comparison this promise sounded too huge to contemplate. It seemed every bit as strange to me as God's word had probably seemed to Mary, especially when our circumstances became much more difficult.

I am just one little mama ministering in the dirt. But I believe that if God can use a donkey, He can use me. I want to be a catalyst for God's glory. I want to believe God can cause His love and glory to shine out of my little laid-down life—and out of your little laid-down life. No matter the cost of saying yes to God, we can respond as Mary did, with a yielded cry of yes.

Thought for Reflection

The Lord still looks for those who will pay all it costs to carry His promises to fruition. Will you?

Prayer

Lord, when the cost of saying yes to You seems high, remind me of what You can do through me if I say am willing. Help me desire to fulfill all that is in Your heart.

DAY 5
YIELDED TO GOD

Mary said, "I am the servant of the Lord.
May it be unto me according to your word."
Then the angel departed from her.
—LUKE 1:38

If you have ever been pregnant or been around a pregnant woman, you know that pregnancy comes with great weight, discomfort, and inconvenience. Carrying the promise of God is a similar experience.

What will you do when carrying God's promise begins to strain you? Will you say, "Please, God, take away the promise! I can't do it anymore. It is too hard. I can't walk this walk. It is too heavy! Give my destiny to someone else." Or will you yield to God, even in the midst of all the radical changes the promise brings—even as it stretches and pulls everything about you into a new shape?

People in the world sometimes abort their

babies because they don't want to make the sacrifices children require. These sacrifices may seem like too great an inconvenience. The price seems too great. The church has sometimes done the same thing with the promises, prophecies, and wooings of God. We have said yes in worship when we felt moved but then aborted what God asked us to carry when things started to feel difficult or inconvenient.

God does not like abortion! It breaks His heart because when we carry that which He placed inside us to full term, His lost sons and daughters—those He planned to reach through our laid-down lives—can come home. He loves to bring in people from darkness. He loves to bring in the lost and the dying and the sick and the broken.

The Lord is looking for those who are so in love with Him that they will say yes when they are wooed and still say yes when great sacrifice is required.

I believe Mary, as she was overshadowed by the Holy Spirit, was engulfed in God's love and might have said to herself, "Though this will cause me incredible pain, though this will cause my reputation to be utterly ruined, though my fiancé may not understand, though my family may disown me, I will carry Your promise to full term, God. I will bear the reproach because I love You. I will carry whatever You place inside of me for love's sake."

What was Mary's response to a seemingly impossible promise? *Yieldedness.*

The Lord can use anyone who will respond to Him as Mary did. He will use anyone who has a willing heart, anyone who will deny himself, anyone who will continue to say yes. Through intimacy with God we can find a place of yielded love in which all fear disappears, a place in which we become willing to do anything and go anywhere for love's sake.

Thought for Reflection

The Lord is looking for those who will yield themselves to Him; He is looking for people who desire to know Him and love Him and are willing to do anything for Him. Do you fit this description? If not, what is holding you back? In what area are you struggling to yield to God?

Prayer

Possess me, Holy Spirit! Let me love like Jesus today. Let me be His fragrance. Let me bring His life. Help me to carry what You have placed within me this day. I love You, Holy Spirit. I love You, Jesus. I love You, Daddy God!

DAY 6
THE EMPOWERMENT
OF THE HOLY SPIRIT

*When the day of Pentecost had come, they were
all together in one place. Suddenly a sound like
a mighty rushing wind came from heaven, and it
filled the whole house where they were sitting. There
appeared to them tongues as of fire, being distributed and resting on each of them, and they were all
filled with the Holy Spirit and began to speak in
other tongues, as the Spirit enabled them to speak.*
—ACTS 2:1–4

Have you ever felt overshadowed by the
Lord? Have you ever been overcome by His
presence? Has the Holy Spirit ever overwhelmed you and changed you forever? On
the Day of Pentecost the Holy Spirit was
given to us, the church. He teaches us, comforts us, and gives us strength and guidance. But He also empowers us to respond
to God's call.

I have felt overshadowed by the Lord several times in my life. The first time was at the age of sixteen. I met Jesus on an Indian reservation in central Mississippi in a Baptist church. The next night I was baptized by the beautiful Holy Spirit at a Pentecostal Holiness church.

Five months later I was worshipping the One who is altogether worthy. The Holy Spirit came, and again I felt overshadowed by Him. During worship the brilliant light of God came, and I was taken up in a vision. I could no longer hear the sermon or anything else around me. This church was extraordinarily loud, but when I felt the Lord descend upon me, all of its many sounds went away. I froze, with my hands up in the air, and then I heard the audible voice of God for the first and only time in my life thus far.

It seemed that Jesus spoke to me, kissing the ring finger on my left hand while oil ran down my arm. I heard Him say, "You will be married to Me. You are called to be a minister and a missionary to Africa, Asia, and England."

I remained stuck in the same position for

three whole hours, kneeling before the Lord without moving, lost in the vision.

That day I discovered a new part of my destiny.

After the overwhelmingly heavy presence of God lifted, I fell apart. I sobbed and I laughed. I have pursued that vision with everything within me for more than three decades since. I have not done anything else. I moved straight ahead as Jesus called me because He ruined me with His love. That visitation so impacted me that I told Jesus I do not care what it costs.

The Holy Spirit can move in our lives in enormous ways. Through the Holy Spirit, God can bring us dreams and visions of the future, and the Holy Spirit can give us the strength and determination to say yes to those visions and dreams no matter the cost. Do you listen for the Holy Spirit in your life?

Thought for Reflection

Do you welcome the presence of the Holy Spirit? Do you let Him overshadow you? Open yourself to Him and see what He wants to do in your life.

Prayer

Lord, overshadow me. Let Your Holy Spirit come and move in my heart and in my life. Teach me to welcome His presence and to receive all the dreams and visions He has for me.

DAY 7
CALLED TO BEAR FRUIT

You are My friends if you do whatever I com-
mand you. I no longer call you servants, for a ser-
vant does not know what his master does. But I
have called you friends, for everything that I have
heard from My Father have I made known to
you. You did not choose Me, but I chose you, and
appointed you, that you should go and bear fruit,
and that your fruit should remain, that the Father
may give you whatever you ask Him in My name.
—JOHN 15:15–16

These are powerful words: God "chose you, and appointed you, that you should go and bear fruit." Do you believe you are called to "bear fruit"? Are you ready to discover how God intends for you to do so?

The day I felt the Lord overshadow me, when He showed me a vision, He planted a promise inside me. This promise was for my future—a future I was to spend serving

Him in Africa, Asia, and England. That day something began growing within me—a call and a ministry.

Some of you may have carried prophetic words for years and yet have never stepped out into them because they seem too costly, too foolish, or too impossible. Maybe you do not feel you are prepared enough, or maybe you are afraid for anyone to know what you feel God said to you because then you might actually be held responsible for acting on His words. Perhaps His promises come with such serious social stigma that you aren't sure you really *want* to carry them.

There may be a steep price for what God has placed in you, but if you want Him, you will choose to pay it. You may have a whole bag of promises, but what are you going to do with them? Will you bear the possible reproach and carry to full term that which God put inside of you? It is easy to hear a great prophetic word but often costly and challenging to bring it to birth.

God has predestined every single one of us for fruitfulness. We need to be familiar with a place of divine intimacy in which we are so consumed by the Holy Spirit that we will nurture and protect the seed He places in us. We need to fearlessly step out and activate His promises. It is intimacy that gives us the grace and strength we need to push through suffering, pain, and inconvenience.

Thought for Reflection

Every one of us was created for a purpose. Every one of us has a call of God on our lives. Have you sought the Lord to find out what your call is? Has anyone ever spoken a prophetic word over you about your future? Consider whether you have been running from the call and why. Then commit to eliminating every wrong thought or action that is holding you back from stepping out to fulfill it.

Prayer

Lord, help me to step out in faith, believing that You have predestined me for fruitfulness. Help me to receive the prophetic words spoken over me and to cooperate with You in bringing them to pass in my life.

DAY 8
BEGIN TODAY

As Jesus walked beside the Sea of Galilee, He saw two brothers, Simon called Peter, and Andrew his brother, throwing a net into the sea, for they were fishermen. And He said to them, "Follow Me, and I will make you fishers of men." They immediately left their nets and followed Him.
—MATTHEW 4:18–20

Are you looking for ways, even today, to begin to fulfill God's calling for you? Look at Peter and Andrew; when Jesus called them, they *immediately* followed Him, stepping into their destiny. I did the same. Even though it took me nearly twenty years to get to Africa, the very day after God gave me the vision telling me I would go to Africa, Asia, and England, I began to step out into my destiny. At that time I had never seen a woman preach. I did not know they could. But I had heard from the Lord that I was to minister, so the next day I started to speak to whoever would listen, loving them in the best way I knew how.

I did not wait for someone to invite me to speak at a church or conference. I found Alzheimer's patients to minister to. They did not remember if I came, and they did not know when I left. They did not look at their watches. I could minister as long as I was led to do so. I also ministered to drug addicts. I sat with them and shared the gospel while they were stoned out of their minds. I asked God to let me pour His love out on them. Even though I was told women did not preach, no one tried to tell me I could not love and speak to drug addicts.

I had the seed of God's promise inside me. Every single friend I had—including my family—thought I was out of my mind. It seemed as if I had lost everyone close to me, but I pressed in for more of God's presence. I told Jesus that I would still trust Him and continue to receive His love and give it away.

Go into the darkness and carry the light God placed inside you. Look for places where people are sad, broken, sick, dying, and desperate. I have been doing that for more than thirty-seven years now. Those are still my favorite kinds of places to be. The broken and dying are always hungry. They are always desperate. They know they are in need.

God is looking for people who will welcome His presence to hover over them freely and who will take steps into their destiny today. He is calling us to say yes to Him, to love Him, and to love His people beginning now.

Thought for Reflection

Can you think of a way to begin today to step into your calling? It's not difficult. Simply love those He puts in front of you with the love of Christ. Whom has He placed in your life that you can minister to?

Prayer

Lord, I want to begin fulfilling my calling where I am, preparing for where You are going to take me. Open opportunities for me to step into. Help me to see the opportunities already around me.

PART 2

THE
SECRET PLACE

DAY 9
SPENDING TIME IN THE SECRET PLACE

Moses took the tent and pitched it outside the camp, a good distance from the camp, and called it the tent of meeting. And anyone who sought the LORD would go out to the tent of meeting which was outside the camp. So whenever Moses went out to the tent, all the people would rise up and stand, every man at the entrance of his tent, and gaze after Moses until he entered the tent. And whenever Moses entered the tent, the pillar of cloud descended and stood at the entrance of the tent, and the LORD spoke with Moses. When all the people saw the pillar of cloud standing at the entrance of the tent, all the people rose up and worshipped, every man at the entrance of his tent. The LORD spoke to Moses face to face, just as a man speaks to his friend. When he returned to the camp, his servant Joshua, the son of Nun, a young man, did not depart from the tent.

—EXODUS 33:7–11

In your daily life spending time in God's presence must be your priority. We all know it is important, but all too often getting alone with the Lord is replaced by our doing things for Him. This is the reverse of the way we ought to approach ministry. To bear fruit for God, we must first spend time with Him.

Moses knew the importance of dwelling in God's presence. He longed to spend time in the secret place. He hungered to be in God's presence so much that he would not move forward without Him. He told God, "How will anyone know that you are pleased with me and with your people unless you go with us?" (Exod. 33:16, NIV). Joshua also knew the importance of dwelling with God in the secret place. We find that when Moses returned to the Israelite camp after God had spoken to him "as a man speaks to his friend," Joshua did not leave the tent. He stayed in God's presence (v. 11).

We too must realize that developing a life in God's presence above all else is the only way to fulfill our God-given destinies. We can do nothing on our own, and we can make no headway in our callings without spending time with Him. Keys to our callings are released when we spend time there. We must always run to Him in the secret place to find the true source of life.

What's more, when we spend time in the secret place, our passion and hunger for Jesus grow. It is only as we abide in His presence that the most precious treasures can be born. This is much better than work! More is accomplished by spending time in God's presence than by doing anything else.

There are no shortcuts to the anointing. If we want to fully walk out the callings the Lord places on our lives, we must spend time with Him, cultivating intimacy in the secret place.

Thought for Reflection

Do you understand the importance of spending time in the secret place, as Moses and Joshua did? Do you live as if fulfilling your God-given calling is a natural outgrowth of the time spent in His presence? Or do you look for shortcuts, trying to fulfill your calling in your own power?

Prayer

Lord, teach me the importance of spending time in the secret place. Help me to realize how much I truly need intimacy with You to fulfill my calling, and cause me to desire time alone with You.

Day 10
Respond to God's Wooing

Listen! I stand at the door and knock. If any-one hears My voice and opens the door, I will come in and dine with him, and he with Me.
—REVELATION 3:20

When God woos you, do you respond to Him? Do you pull you away from your work and other responsibilities to spend time alone with Him?

There is a time for wooing, and there is a time for work. It is important to know the difference. We all need to work. However, when God begins wooing us, it is important to recognize it's time to cease working and enter into His glorious presence.

I work very hard. I am a very responsible person. But there are moments when God draws me to Himself even closer, and He asks me to come away from all of the activity and spend time alone with Him. The only thing that truly satisfies me is being in His presence, and it is His wooing that brings me to a place of surrender. In holy surrender I find all the strength I need to run the race.

In fact, I don't know how to run the race without the wooing. Without romance I cannot be a minister. I have tried before—I just cannot do it. I do not even want to. But when I am in love, I will run eighteen hours a day. I will run after Him with everything inside me, and I will be at rest, even as I am running.

In this life we can run ourselves to exhaustion doing more and more things for God without ever understanding what He really desires from us. God longs to increase our appetite for Him. If we will eat and drink of Him, He will bring us into the relationship that will transform us into His likeness. We will begin to eat and drink of Jesus so deeply every day that we no longer grow weary or get exhausted as we run our race. We will learn to simply live in the secret place of His heart continually.

People often ask me what the secret to sustainability is. The secret place is the secret; spending time away from distractions and with Him is the secret. We have to live there. If you think you know how to live in the secret place but there is no fruit in your life, you have not been there. To the degree that we are united with God's heart and in love with Jesus, we will be fruitful.

When I talk to my coworkers, I always emphasize this same thing. Over and over again I say, "All fruitfulness flows from intimacy." I always remind our team that intimacy is the only way to bear fruit that lasts. I watch those who have learned the mystery of the secret place too. They understand that when they seek more time with God, they will bear far more fruit and will have the grace to keep running, even in the midst of great pressure. They thrive over the years because they have learned to abide in the realm where we are all called to live.

Thought for Reflection

Do you regularly spend time in the secret place? Do you carve out time in your schedule to meet with God daily? To fulfill His call on your life and to be able to consistently say yes to God, you must spend time in the secret place seeking His face and His desires for you. Think about how you can make this a priority in your life.

Prayer

Lord, help me to respond when I sense that You want to spend more time with me. Let me know when You are calling me, wooing me into Your presence. I want You to woo me. Help me be open to it.

DAY 11
THE SECRET TO
DIVINE STRATEGIES

Call to Me, and I will answer you, and show you
great and mighty things which you do not know.
—JEREMIAH 33:3

Do you want to know how to fulfill your
calling? God is the one who has given it to
you, and He has a strategy for you to fulfill it.
Seeking that strategy is the only way to discover the fullness of His plan for you.

Before you move forward in the ministry
the Lord has called you to, it is important
to seek Him and spend time in the secret
place until He reveals His strategy. Don't
attempt to do anything you do not see in
His Word or have not sensed in His presence. As Proverbs says, "Lean not on your
own understanding...acknowledge Him,
and He will direct your paths" (Prov. 3:5–6).
This is true in your ministry as well as in

every other aspect of your life. Even Jesus, the Son of God, did only what He saw the Father doing (John 5:19).

I have a confession to make: I have no idea how to prepare for conferences and meetings. I simply live in communion with God, where fruitfulness can flow. Preparing my life to overflow is the only way I know how to prepare.

When the Lord first showed me the revival that would come to Mozambique, I had planned for our ministry to take in only a few hundred more children. I thought that was the best we could do because we did not have many fathers for them, only mothers and other young adults. Not long afterward God gave us a fresh strategy to go with the vision. He spoke to us and said He was going to touch the hearts of the fathers to care for the children and bring them into their own homes.

We believed God, and now there is an extraordinary movement. From the communities where they have planted churches, many pastors are taking in children who need care. Most of these children are cared for in the homes of these pastors or by widows and others in those same communities.

Without the divine strategy the Lord showed us, our ministry never would have experienced such growth, and these children wouldn't have homes or families. You must seek the Lord's plan to fulfill the call on your life.

Thought for Reflection

Are you trying to follow your own plan and strategy for fulfilling the dreams and visions God has placed inside of you for your future? Or do you spend time seeking Him and His strategy to bring these dreams into reality? Do you believe that He gave them to you and will bring them to pass as you cooperate with Him?

Prayer

Lord, help me to seek You for all that I need to bring the dreams and visions within me into reality. Prevent me from going my own direction, and teach me to do only what I see You doing. Show me how to remain in communion with You so that the life of God overflows from within me as I carry out Your strategies.

Day 12
Responding to God's Direction

*My sheep hear My voice, and I know
them, and they follow Me.*
—JOHN 10:27

As you spend time in the secret place and God gives you insights into His strategy for you, you must make plans to act on those insights. Knowing the Lord intimately is the first step, but acting on what He tells you is just as important.

The truth is, we cannot step out and transform any place for God unless we carry what He calls us to carry. When we live in His presence, nations begin to change, one person at a time. Whether God sends you to a vast multitude or to twenty-five people, He has called you to be significant. He has called each of us to live in His presence and to stop for the one He puts in front of us each day.

God wants to use us, but we have to believe and act upon the revelations He gives us in the secret place.

For instance, Rolland and I had a vision to go to a nation. What would have happened, though, if we had not bought the plane tickets? What if we hadn't wanted to lay our lives down? What if we hadn't lived in God's presence? What if we'd been given this great vision for the poor and the sick but did nothing? What if we hadn't gotten in the Land Rover and spent all those days, weeks, and months driving to unreached villages, at times getting stuck in the mud? What if we hadn't wanted to release the work of that vision to so many hundreds of others? What if we'd tried to do it ourselves?

Our hearts might have been filled with nice revelations, but nothing would have happened if we and our Iris family had not believed Him and responded. Without belief that manifested itself in action, none of that vision would have come through our lives and the lives of those in our movement. We must respond to what God shows us in the secret place—not just for our sake, but also for the sake of all those He wants to touch through us.

When God tells us to do something while we are in His presence, we need to respond. We need to go and do what He says. Jesus said, "The Son can do nothing of Himself, but what He sees the Father do" (John 5:19). In His presence God breaks our hearts and opens our eyes to see what He is doing all around us. That is why we cannot go anywhere without His being present in our lives. If we remain in the secret place, it is first of all because we love Him, and it is also because we are like little children and must watch Him as He shows us what to do.

Thought for Reflection

Has God given you a strategy that you haven't yet acted on? What is holding you back? The call God has placed on your life cannot be fulfilled without taking action. Give your fears, insecurities, and worries over to God now, so you can begin to enact His divine strategy.

Prayer

Lord, now that I have Your strategy to fulfill the dreams You have placed in me, help me to act on it. Let nothing step in my way as I work to fulfill the call You have placed on my life.

DAY 13
LIVING IN GOD'S PRESENCE

Moses said to the LORD, "See, You say to me, 'Bring up this people,' but You have not let me know whom You will send with me. Yet You have said, 'I know you by name, and you have also found grace in My sight.' Now therefore, I pray You, if I have found favor in Your sight, show me now Your way, that I may know You, and that I may find favor in Your sight. Consider too that this nation is Your people."

And He said, "My Presence will go with you, and I will give you rest."

Then he said to Him, "If Your Presence does not go with us, do not bring us up from here."
—EXODUS 33:12–15

God can qualify whomever He likes whenever He likes. He can use any yielded lover and any yielded vessel. However, Moses demanded God's presence before he acted. That is why God was pleased to use him—he told God he was not going anywhere without

His presence (Exod. 33:15). I believe the favor of God on Moses increased the very moment he said yes and that he would not do God's bidding without God's presence. God was looking for a man who would not depend on his own ability, and Moses knew his task was impossible without God's help. He yielded to God's leading because he knew there was no other way to accomplish the task.

This same truth applies to us today. God is pleased to use us as we ask for His presence to go with us.

One day, as I was resting in the secret place, the Lord gave me a vision of freshwater wells and a particular church. Then I felt Him call us to drill wells and put them near the churches. We bought two well-drilling rigs, but no one could get them to work. It was pitiful. The means to this great vision were sitting around doing absolutely nothing. We had no technician, no help, not even the keys to start up the rigs.

For two years we contended to see the vision of the wells become a reality. Problem after problem arose until I told God I could not do it alone—just as Moses knew he could not do what God had called him to do by himself (Exod. 33:12). Together we continued to trust in God's promise of living water springing forth, spiritually and physically.

At last hope came when a friend of ours told us he knew an engineer who was going to help. His name was David. The hope was fleeting, however, because David had never finished high school and had never dug a well. But he told me he believed God said he was the man for the job. David got the rigs working, and wells were dug despite his education level and lack of experience.

In just a few days God used David to accomplish a mission that had been disrupted for years. God sent us a man who believed what was spoken to him in the secret place. He trusted God would give him the ability he needed. He heard God and acted. Thousands of people are now drinking fresh, clean water because one yielded vessel said yes.

As we step out in obedience, our most stubborn prayer ought to be, "God, I will do anything You tell me to do—but You have to go with me. I will not live in complacency because of my lack of ability. I will yield myself to You. I trust that You will make me able."

Thought for Reflection

The Holy Spirit can do incredible things through a person who is yielded to God's will, who is willing to say yes and to trust that God will work through him. Following God's divine strategy may not be easy, and there may be problems, but it's important to say yes anyway. Will you continue to say yes and continue to trust until the vision is fulfilled?

Prayer

Lord, help me to know that You can fulfill the dreams and visions I have no matter what I bring to the table. You qualify those who are called, regardless of their background or circumstances. Qualify me, Lord. Use me. And let Your presence go with me, no matter what the task.

DAY 14
REMAIN IN THE SECRET PLACE

Then he said to Him, "If Your Presence does not go with us, do not bring us up from here. For how will it be known that I have found favor in Your sight, I and Your people? Is it not by Your going with us, so that we will be distinguished, I and Your people, from all the people who are on the face of the earth?"

The LORD said to Moses, "I will do this thing of which you have spoken, for you have found favor in My sight, and I know you by name."
—EXODUS 33:15–17

The Lord was pleased with Moses because he would not consent to lead Israel without His continual presence. When we abide in God's presence, the striving and fear in our souls go away. Moses told God, "Now therefore, I pray You, if I have found favor in Your sight, show me now Your way, that I may know You, and that I may find favor in Your sight. Consider too that this nation is Your people" (Exod. 33:13). The Lord replied to him, "My Presence will go with you, and I will give you rest" (v. 14). Then the Lord told Moses what He says to all who are yielded, laid-down lovers—that He will do the very thing we asked because He is pleased with us and knows us by name (v. 17).

Continually spending time with Him in the secret place is a necessity; it leads you to hear the Lord's desires for you. One day I was walking through a village in Mozambique, and I noticed a very old lady in rags sitting in the dirt against a mud hut. She was blind. I felt the Lord asking me to stop for her.

In the local dialect I asked her what her name was. She told me she had none. I thought perhaps she was from another tribe and didn't understand my Makua dialect. I asked her again in a different language, but her answer was the same: "I am blind. I have no name."

I was stunned. I hugged the old blind woman and immediately decided that I would call her Utaliya. It means "you exist" or "you are." When I spoke it for the first time, her wrinkled face came alive. She gave me a huge, nearly toothless grin. I asked another woman nearby to try calling her by the new name. Utaliya turned her white, blind eyes toward that unfamiliar sound and giggled. After that I prayed for her eyes. I watched them turn brown in front of me.

Utaliya could see! I told her about the man Jesus who had just opened her eyes. I told her about Papa Daddy God, who will always call her by name. She met God that day.

God is pleased to use anyone who believes in Him, but how will you know when He wants to use you if you don't spend time with Him? It is the relationship and intimacy that grows out of remaining in Him that allows you to know His heart, to know when He is calling you to stop for one such as Utaliya. He longs to release the keys and strategies from heaven to us in the secret place. His method for changing your nation is *you*. You are the salt. You are the light. You are the person He wants to use.

Thought for Reflection

Remaining in the secret place allows God to use you in deeper ways. Do you insist on His being present to you before you begin your work each day? Do you spend quality time with Him so that you can sense when He is calling you to stop for those who need Him?

Prayer

Lord, I want to abide in the secret place. I want to know You deeply and intimately. I want to know, without a doubt, when You are asking me to stop for one in need, and I want to know how to help him. I know Your guidance and direction will come; draw me into Your presence so I will spend time with You until it comes.

DAY 15
STAY THIRSTY

O God, You are my God; early will I seek You;
my soul thirsts for You, my flesh faints for You, in
a dry and thirsty land with no water....My soul
clings hard to You; Your right hand upholds me.
—PSALM 63:1, 8

The sentiments expressed by King David in Psalm 63 must be our sentiments. If we want to be fruitful, we must be in a continual state of hunger and thirst for God, desirous of spending time with Him, and joyfully seeking Him at every opportunity.

It is important to remain thirsty and to remember God wants to use you. He intends to equip you with His Word and His presence. This is not a one-time event. It is not like walking into a scheduled meeting from which you can carry away all you will ever require. Becoming familiar with God's Word and His presence is a lifelong journey. The more you experience them, the more desperately you will need them.

Most of us have had a vision, calling, or dream from God at one time in our lives. It is likely that not all of what God has shown us has come to pass. If we are to accomplish all He wants for us in this life, we must always desire more of Him. There is always room for more intimacy, more of His presence, and more of His glory.

Our passion will continue to live and burn as long as we cultivate a holy hunger, positioning ourselves to be overshadowed again and again, looking deep into the eyes of Jesus and eating of Him each day.

I pray that you would be drawn to feast upon God's goodness in the secret place and that you would rest in Him at such a deep level that yielding to His will becomes easy. May you be one who is not content to go anywhere without His presence. May you "seek His face continually" (1 Chron. 16:11). In all challenges and all victories I pray that you would seek and find Him. I pray that from within His heart, you would see and stop for each one He places before you. I pray you would live a life of abundant fruitfulness, flowing from intimacy in the secret place.

Thought for Reflection

Do you desire more of God? Do you take the time to rest in Him at a deep level each day? What will it require for you to cultivate a continual hunger and thirst for His presence?

Prayer

Lord, I am thirsty for You. Please help me to remain thirsty. The more I have of You, the closer I am, and the more I want. Please, Lord, let that never change. Let me be ever thirsty, ever seeking—and ever growing in intimacy with You.

DAY 16
PURE IN HEART

Consider how much love the Father has given to us,
that we should be called children of God. Therefore
the world does not know us, because it did not know
Him. Beloved, now are we children of God, and it
has not yet been revealed what we shall be. But we
know that when He appears, we shall be like Him,
for we shall see Him as He is. Everyone who has
this hope in Him purifies himself, just as He is pure.
—1 JOHN 3:1–3

As we spend time in the secret place, hungry for His presence and His work in our lives, we will feel the call to purity. When I meditate on how God intended us to be "pure in heart," I think of the words of Mother Teresa: "To love with a pure heart, to love everybody, especially to love the poor, is a twenty-four-hour prayer."[1]

Loving the poor is truly a full-time job, but it is one filled with tremendous joy. I am daily challenged when the needs are so great, the queues so long, and the multitudes so hungry. Among the poor in Africa we are seeing revival fueled and sustained by the power of God in spite of all our weaknesses. His mercies and compassions never fail; they are new every morning.

When I think of what God requires to be pure in heart, I think of my beautiful Mozambican children. These children are my delight as they hunger for more of Jesus. They are my mentors, and they have helped to teach me not to be led astray from the simplicity and purity of devotion. Sometimes we make things too complicated when we really need to remember that the kingdom belongs to the children!

When He appears, we shall be like Him! We shall see as He sees and feel as He feels. But we do not have to wait until we get to heaven to let Him purify us. We must cry out to be purified and freed from every hidden agenda, rotten motive, and false assumption about God.

My heart's one desire is to be holy in love. I long for the purifying fire of His love to consume every hidden motive within me. As the heart is purified, we can see Him with greater and greater clarity. I want to be fully possessed by His Holy Spirit until I am completely overshadowed by God. I want to be utterly overtaken.

My prayer is for all of us to stay hidden inside God's glorious heart of love until we are manifesting His nature as sons and daughters, living, breathing, moving, healing, and life-giving, just as Jesus was. As we are purified, we will see God more clearly. As our hearts become pure, our vision becomes clearer.

Thought for Reflection

What do you think it means to be "pure in heart"? Do you long to manifest God's nature in this area?

Prayer

Lord, as I stay in the secret place and abide in You, purify my heart. I want to be free from every personal agenda so that I may love others as You love them.

DAY 17
GOD PURIFIES OUR HEARTS

*Purify me with hyssop, and I will be
clean; wash me, and I will be whiter than
snow.... Create in me a clean heart, O
God, and renew a right spirit within me.*
—PSALM 51:7, 10

When we spend time in the secret place, the Lord will purify our hearts. The best example I remember of this was what He did with one of my Mozambican sons, Aurio. He had a vision of Jesus's face that expanded his capacity to love. Aurio is a picture for me of how God can purify our hearts. He is a half-caste child whom I found dying in the trash. He was trying to survive by scavenging from one of the world's poorest garbage dumps. I knew that there was something very special about this little boy.

Aurio was full of demons. As a small child he could easily throw several pastors off himself. I did not know anything else to do for him but to hold him in my arms and pray quietly for his heart to be healed.

One day as we were worshipping in our church tent in Zimpeto, I watched as Aurio lay facedown in the sand, sobbing and worshipping God. He was crying and shaking—he was desperate for God. Hour after hour our Mozambican aunties who oversee the children were getting more and more nervous. They finally came to me as I was preaching and said, "Mama Aida, what should we do?"

I said, "It's good what's happening to him. I understand because I have been on the floor myself for days at a time. I know what it means to be there. His weeping is a sign of a holy visitation. Leave him alone there; God is touching him." Of all the children whom God could have chosen, He had handpicked this little one—the one most broken, most hungry, who loved God with all his heart.

The next day as I was playing with the little girls, Aurio saw me and came bolting toward me. When he jumped into my arms, I said, "You are absolutely radiant!"

He said, "Mama Aida, I saw Jesus!"

Today Aurio shares the good news from a flatbed truck with the poor who live in the bush. He is so full of life and light. When he looks out on a crowd of even a thousand or more in an unreached people group, he is not intimidated. Although his heart still aches for his lost parents, since that visitation he knows he is a son of the house. He knows signs and wonders are not reserved for the spiritual elite.

The heart of the Father beats inside of Aurio as he preaches with joy. He sings and worships God, and when people throw stones at him, he does not care. When he lays hands on the sick, they are often healed.

I have watched as that child who was once the most rejected now lives with the light of God's glory and burns brightly with the fire of God's love. And I have watched him work through painful issues by the grace of God. Something happened during that visitation that increased Aurio's capacity to love and forgive. God took his heart of stone and gave him a heart of flesh. (See Ezekiel 36:26.)

Thought for Reflection

God can purify your heart just as He did Aurio's. He can touch and increase your capacity to love. How can you open yourself up to Him today?

Prayer

Father, purify my heart. Reveal Yourself to me and turn my world upside-down with Your love. Help me to see myself not as an outsider but as one of Your children whom You cherish.

PART 3

DEEPER STILL

Day 18
Called to Go Deep

*When the man who had the line in his hand went
eastward, he measured a thousand cubits, and he
brought me through the water; the water reached the
ankles. Again he measured a thousand and brought
me through the water. The water reached the knees.
Again he measured a thousand and brought me
through the water. The water reached the loins.*

—EZEKIEL 47:3–4

When you are a skilled diver, you can
choose how deep you will go when you hit
the water. You can simply skim the surface,
you can glide just beneath, or you can plumb
the depths. In a similar way, we have a choice
about how deeply we wish to dive into God.

God is calling us to go deep in Him. He is
entreating us to let Him have complete control. He is inviting us to dive deeper into the
river of His presence so we can experience
true life, to come to a place where our life is

not our own and where we can be immersed in the river of life that flows from His Spirit.

Ezekiel knew what it meant to go deeper. The waters into which he was invited poured straight from the temple of God, and we also are called to enter them. The source of the river is God Himself.

God is asking which of us wants to go deeper. Constantly He calls us to greater and greater depths, inviting us to sink down until the river covers us completely and makes our hearts glad.

The angel of the Lord invited Ezekiel to come deeper and deeper still into the water. He measured out a line. Ezekiel was likely very frightened by this invitation. Who knows if he could swim or not? When we are ankle-deep in water, we control everything. We can swish and walk around and continue to maintain our balance. We can do ministry our own way. We prefer this because we like to be in charge. I know how frightening it can be to feel as if you might be drowning.

But I have been sharing the gospel ceaselessly and passionately for more than thirty-seven years, and in that time I have learned that you cannot do very much while you are only ankle-deep in the river of God. When you are only ankle-deep, you may still know the Holy Spirit. You may have profound convictions. You may have charismatic gifts. You may see some of God's power. Even so, most of the time you will be confined to activities you know how to produce and control. You will be walking on your own and relying on your own plans.

Now I always press in to go in deeper. Continually I ask God to take me deep and drown me in His river. God offers an invitation to all who are thirsty to be fully immersed in the glory of His love.

Thought for Reflection

Does the thought of being fully immersed in the river scare you? Does the idea of letting go and allowing God to have full control make you nervous? What will it take for you to go deeper in God?

Prayer

Father God, show me that I can trust You. Show me that giving You full control will bring me closer and increase my fruitfulness for Your kingdom.

DAY 19
GOING DEEP MEANS GOING LOW

Pride goes before destruction, and a haughty spirit before a fall. Better it is to be of a humble spirit with the lowly than to divide the spoil with the proud.
—PROVERBS 16:19

Have you ever been high up in the mountains or at the top of a canyon and seen a river far down below you? The rivers are always in the valleys, running in the lowly places, to places that are even lower still.

One day Jesus showed me a vision. He said, "I want to take you up the mountain to a low place because the river flows to the low places." Just as natural rivers always flow into low places, so the river of God always flows into the lowly places. In order to enter it, we have to go lower and lower still. We have to go down into the valley, humbling ourselves, to reach the depths that God offers to us.

We are called to go low so that we can go deep into God's presence. When we are bent down, kneeling down, bowed down, and laid down—then we will find Him. When we humble ourselves and live lives of humility, we can find God. First Peter 5:5 says, "God resists the proud, but gives grace to the humble." Luke 1:52 says, "He has brought down rulers from their thrones but has lifted up the humble." Perhaps we must be low enough to live in God's glory.

If we are low enough in the Spirit, we will recognize even a trickle of God's presence in a room. Once we are in this place of humility and lowliness, we certainly will not be concerned with our position, our place, or anything else that might hinder us. Our overwhelming desire will be full immersion in the river. Nothing else will matter.

You should want to be immersed in, and live inside, the very heart of God. From there, all fruitfulness flows.

I am learning to live in that place of "lower still." The question for all of us is this: How low do we want to go? How laid down—yielded—do we want to be? I believe we have a choice about how deeply we wish to dive in to God, and it depends on how low we are willing to go, how humbled we will become.

Thought for Reflection

Are you learning to live in the place of "lower still"? Do you seek to be so humbled before the Lord that you no longer care about your position in life? It is in this place, where nothing else matters, that you begin to dive into God's presence. Are you ready?

Prayer

Father, help me to repent of my pride. Help me to humble myself before You. I want to be in the place where nothing matters other than You and Your presence. I want to experience You.

DAY 20
DEEPER STILL

*Truly, truly I say to you, unless a grain of
wheat falls into the ground and dies, it remains
alone. But if it dies, it bears much fruit.*
—JOHN 12:24

I believe we were created to live under the
waters of the Holy Spirit. In fact, I feel as if
I was born to be in the water. I matured in
a way opposite that of a frog. At the beginning frogs start out as tadpoles, swimming
under the water, and grow up to live on land.
I went the other direction. I was like a frog,
living on land, and then I became a tadpole. I
changed from breathing the air of the world
to needing the waters of the Spirit.

For years Rolland and I were about waist-
deep. We had a total of one very wobbly
church to show for it. I imagine frogs can hop
in waist-deep water. They have strong legs. I
certainly hopped as high as I could for Jesus.

I tried so hard to make everything work that my head spun and my heart grew weary.

Then the Lord said, "Come on deeper," and we got one more wobbly church. He said again, "Come on deeper," and we got another wobbly church. Now we had three wobbly churches. We were still hopping with all our might, but we could get only so far being waist-deep in His presence.

Then God showed me an easier way. He showed me I could die to myself. Then He would kiss me back to life, and everything would change.

I believe the Lord is calling us to a lifestyle of laid-down love that goes well beyond being waist-deep in the river. It is a permanent lifestyle of "lower still." It is a call to dive into a love that is limitless, ceaseless, and bottomless—a call to relinquish control.

"Deeper still" is a place of both death and life. The Lord wants to love you to death and kiss you to life. But this cannot happen by your own strength or design. It is exclusively the gift of an intimate relationship with Him.

It is when you become immersed in the love of the Father that you truly begin to love like Jesus. He wants to immerse you. He wants to hold you. He wants to take you to a place where you are so far over your head in the river of God that miracles happen all around you. He wants to fill you entirely with His Holy Spirit.

Thought for Reflection

Do you want to live in the ankle-deep presence of God, or do you want to be immersed in Him? Do you want to keep striving to do things for God through your own effort, or do you want to learn how to swim? Do you want to be so fully immersed in His presence that you begin to see what burns on His heart? If so, will you allow yourself to be confronted with His pain over the world's multitudes of lost, lonely, hungry, and dying people?

Prayer

Lord, when You call me deeper, help me to respond. Help me dive in, giving up my desire for control so that I may have a deeper relationship with You.

Day 21
How Deep Will You Go?

*Afterward he measured a thousand. And
it was a river that I could not pass over, for
the water had risen, enough water to swim
in, a river that could not be passed over.*
—EZEKIEL 47:5

How deep in this river did Ezekiel want to go? Ankle-deep, waist-deep, neck-deep? Did he long to go all the way in? In the end the angel of the Lord took Ezekiel into a river too deep to cross. The current was too powerful and the waters too high for him to have any stability besides the Lord.

Diving all the way into the river means we have no more ability to stand on our own. There is nowhere to set our feet. It takes complete surrender. And God wants to take us beyond what we can control. He wants to take us to a place where we can be moved in any direction purely by the flow of His presence.

Anyone who has ever worked in our ministry understands we are in way over our heads. It bothers some people. In fact, we are so in over our heads that if God does not show up through supernatural provision, people will go hungry. Every day thousands of children look to us for their daily meals. We cannot continue to provide for them without divine intervention. We literally have to trust God our Father for our daily bread. We have no backup plan. We simply keep leaning deeper and deeper into the goodness of the Lord.

Whenever I am home in Pemba, I like to swim out in the ocean. It is one of my favorite ways to get into the secret place. Beneath the water it is easy to feel hidden in God. There are no distractions.

I try to get as far from shore as I can. If anyone spots me and tries to chase me, I swim faster. If they yell my name, I go where I cannot hear them anymore. If I am going to be good for anything during the rest of the week, I absolutely require this time. I stay desperate for that time with God.

Under the waves I ask God to teach me how I can live in the river without interruption. I want to be fully immersed in the Holy Spirit. I want to be completely covered until no one will see me but only Christ in me. As John 3:30 says, "He must increase, but I must decrease." Even in that place, when I am totally hidden and the Holy Spirit fills each breath, I long to go deeper still.

Thought for Reflection

Are you ready to dive deep into the waters of the Holy Spirit? Do you live as if you must decrease while He increases? Do you always long to go deeper, no matter how deep you are? Think about what it will take for you to surrender fully to the Lord.

Prayer

Lord, prepare me to dive deep into my relationship with You. Prepare me to be in a place where reliance on You is absolutely necessary. I want to be that deep; I want to be that close to You.

DAY 22
DROWNING IN HIS LOVE

I have been crucified with Christ. It is no longer I
who live, but Christ who lives in me. And the life
I now live in the flesh, I live by faith in the Son
of God, who loved me and gave Himself for me.
—GALATIANS 2:20

Have you ever been scuba diving? Believe
it or not, it can be a spiritual experience.

I love to scuba dive, and I like to go as
far down toward the reefs as I can. When I
dive, I have to strap on weights so I can stay
underwater without effort; if I don't wear
weights, I'll have to constantly kick my legs,
swimming downward to keep from floating
back to the surface.

The glory of the Lord can sometimes feel
like a heavy weight, and that very weight is a
gift. It helps us sink low into the deep places
and stay there without strain. Without the

heavy glory of the Lord upon us, we cannot find the lowest place.

When I dive, I get to experience a new and different realm. Through my mask a different world greets me, like another dimension. God's kingdom too is a different realm, and when He calls us there, He is calling us to a new dimension.

One day the Lord spoke right as I stepped off the dry land and into the ocean. I felt Him say, "It's that easy to live in the realm of the kingdom. Is this deep enough for you?"

I said, "No, Lord."

Then I felt Him say, "Come deeper still."

I stepped farther into the water over shallow rocks and sand. I waded in until I was up to my waist and felt Him say, "Now allow Me to carry you." I let myself go all the way into the water. Just like that another reality covered and surrounded me.

Allowing God to carry us when we don't understand what's happening can feel frightening. Sometimes we may feel as if we're about to drown. He comforts us only by promising that when we let go, we actually will die. After death, however, there is new resurrection life. Even after coming to know Jesus as our Savior, there remains a place of "deeper still." We can go on to become totally immersed in the realm of our Father's love.

Some may hesitate, make excuses, and step away because the prospect of immersion looks dangerous. Some will think they are not ready to swim that far down and will wonder why they're being thrown into deep water when they don't even know how to swim. I believe that the Lord would tell you not to worry. If you jump in, He will catch you, and then you will drown in His deep love. Whenever we do choose to jump, He will pull us right down so we are forced to learn how to breathe in the Holy Spirit's realm.

Thought for Reflection

If we die to ourselves, we will experience the resurrection life of Christ. We may be frightened to let go, but when we do, God carries us into the depths of His love and teaches us to breathe in the realm of the Spirit. Let this thought bring you peace as you prepare to be immersed in the river of His presence.

Prayer

Lord, let me die to myself to live for You. I want to dive into Your presence and find new life in Your love. It is scary, but it is worth it. Help me to trust You.

DAY 23
BREATHING UNDERWATER

Yet the hour is coming, and is now here, when
the true worshippers will worship the Father in
spirit and truth. For the Father seeks such to wor-
ship Him. God is Spirit, and those who worship
Him must worship Him in spirit and truth.
—JOHN 4:23–24

God is calling us to be a people who can breathe underwater. We have kept our heads above water long enough. Being in over our heads and out of control is precisely what He wants.

I feel that the Lord is inviting us into a place we have been afraid to live in—the supernatural realm of His kingdom, where His manifest presence surrounds and holds us like water in the ocean's depths. We were created to breathe in this realm; we were created to worship Him, to live in His presence.

We can be permanently immersed in the glory of His love. We simply have to drown.

God wants to accustom you to a different realm because your real home is not here; it is in heaven (Phil. 3:20). Being in the African bush is an unspeakable joy for me, but it is not my home. My heart is with the One I love. I spend so much of my life trying to swim down deeper that the reality of this earth is not mine anymore.

God is looking for people He can so immerse in His love that for the rest of their lives they will have to survive inside His heart. Nothing else will matter to them. In this secret place you can hear the heartbeat of God for yourself. He will tell you the things that delight His heart. He will call you to go and to do whatever He wants, and you will not refuse Him.

He knows it is frightening. Still, He calls us deeper. No matter how deep we have gone, there is more. We need to go deeper and lower until all we have is the mind of Christ. We are called to be more than a people who can dive for brief periods but have to keep popping up our heads, trying to figure it all out. We have to be able to breathe in His atmosphere without coming up for the world's air.

Thought for Reflection

Ask God to immerse you in His love until the only thing you understand is His heart. Worship Him and wait upon Him until you are overwhelmed to the point of no return. If you drink daily from the river of God and stay immersed in Him, then with increasing measure you will begin to pour out a love that is irresistible. As you minister to the broken, the dying, and the hurting, God's holy presence will overflow and spill forth with peace and joy through every part of your life.

Prayer

God, I'm not satisfied. I cannot live ankle-, knee-, or waist-deep. I must be completely immersed in Your presence. Lord, here I am. Immerse me. I do not want to keep from drowning. I want to drown in Your love. I want to know what it is to be immersed and undone. I want to know what it is for me not to be in control and for You to be totally and completely in control. Lord, come like a rushing river. I invite You to sweep me away to deeper places each day.

DAY 24
BRINGING LIFE TO
THE DARK PLACES

He said to me, "Son of man, have you seen this?"

*Then he brought me and caused me to return to
the brink of the river. When I had returned I
saw on the bank of the river very many trees on
the one side and on the other. Then he said to
me, "This water flows toward the eastern region
and goes down into the valley, and enters the sea.
When it flows into the sea, the water will become
fresh. Every living creature that swarms, wherever the rivers go, will live. And there shall be a
very great multitude of fish, because these waters
shall come there and the others become fresh. Thus
everything shall live wherever the river comes."*
—EZEKIEL 47:6–9

Sometimes it is difficult to understand, but
trials and challenging times are a part of life,
even for Christians—and God can use them
for our benefit. I'll give you a good example.

A great outpouring in my nation of Mozambique began in the midst of a flood that brought vast destruction. It was so bad in the villages that there were instances of women having to give birth to their babies in trees. We went out with helicopters, Land Rovers, and boats to help as many as we could. When we had to, we went wading through the water on foot.

As we did this, hundreds of thousands of people started coming to Jesus. People were desperate. This terrible flood brought one of the greatest spiritual changes the land has ever seen. Before the Mozambique floods we used to lead people to the Lord a few at a time. Now they come in swarms. Often almost whole villages received Jesus overnight.

Sometimes God will allow you to wait and wonder why He is not doing something exactly when you thought He would. But He knows what He is doing. God is very much in control even if His way of doing things is unexpected. That is why we stay under the river's waters.

His river flows through us as a consequence of the intimate love found in the secret place. We have to enter this river for ourselves in order to get to the life that is found there. Once we are immersed in His river, life will also follow us wherever we go—even into the darkest of places.

When we live in the river of God, totally immersed in His heart, healing is released through us. Rich life springs up along the banks and the shores of our lives. Pure water from God transforms and purifies any other murky waters we may face. It makes salty or bitter waters fresh.

When we went from three churches to thousands of churches in a few short years, it was because God immersed us in His Spirit in a way we had never known before. He looked at us—little people laid down in the dirt so low that even the smallest stream of His presence would have been able to flow over our heads—and He blessed us all. He poured out His Holy Spirit and sent a host of beautiful ministers to our movement. As it says in the Ezekiel passage, swarms of creatures and fish were found in this river.

God has given us a powerful promise: wherever the river flows, life will thrive. Imagine abundant life, healing, and joy released without measure in every place we set our feet. I believe that is exactly what is to come as we learn, together, to abide in the river.

Thought for Reflection

Think about God's promise that wherever the river flows, there will be life. Do you want to be responsible for helping to bring that life? Do you want to be an agent of salvation, healing, and joy without measure? What is it that keeps you from abiding in the river of God so that you can fulfill this call?

Prayer

Lord, help me to understand that You are in control even in the midst of the floods of life. Help me to see Your hand at work and to trust You to bring good out of them. Most of all, help me to remain in the river so that Your life will flow through me no matter what I am going through.

DAY 25
SPREAD WIDE YOUR NETS

*It shall come to pass that the fishermen shall stand
upon it. From En Gedi even to En Eglaim there
shall be a place to spread out nets. Their fish shall
be according to their kinds, as the fish of the Medi-
terranean Sea, exceedingly many....By the river
upon its bank, on this side and on that side, shall
grow all kinds of trees for food, whose leaf shall
not fade nor shall its fruit fail. They shall bring
forth fruit according to their months, because their
water issues out of the sanctuary. And their fruit
shall be for food and their leaves for medicine.*
—EZEKIEL 47:10, 12

God calls us to bear fruit in abundance—
just like the trees in Ezekiel's prophecy. But
we are not called to do His work alone.

We can take a lesson from the fishermen
of Pemba. They are always spreading fishing
nets in front of our children's base in Mozambique, which is located right on the ocean.

Usually ten to twenty women will spread a single massive net. These nets are far too big for any one person to handle. They get covered in weights to anchor them to the ocean floor, and at the end of the day I watch the people come back and sing together as they haul in the catch. Because they work together, the process looks effortless.

Working in the Father's kingdom is like those women spreading the net. Working together, under the Father's love, makes our efforts fruitful and easier.

There are "fish" all around us, waiting to be captured in the net of the Father's love. Horrible things have happened in this generation, but that is all the more reason to spread our nets in faith and believe that we are going to bring in multitudes.

Our time for taking up a fishing pole and waiting three hours to catch one fish is over. It is a time for us to cooperate in laying down the vast nets God has placed in our hands. We do not need to strive to the breaking point. We simply need to be hidden inside His heart and work together. I believe He is raising up an army of laid-down lovers who will each hold on to his or her part of the net in order to bring in fish by the millions.

The trees rooted on the banks of the river flowing from the sanctuary of God bear fruit every month of the year. This is a supernatural process. If we stay immersed, God will cause us to yield fruit at a supernatural pace.

Fruitfulness is birthed from love. Bearing fruit is a delight, but it is not the final goal. Intimacy with God must be our purpose. If we pursue Him above all else, fruit simply happens. I have never seen a fruit tree push hard and say, "Give me fruit!" Trees have no other task than to stand rooted in the soil. They soak up the waters that flow from the heart of God, and new life grows.

The person who gives control to God opens himself to the possibility of untimely fruitfulness. Those who choose this way lay their whole lives upon the altar, willing to be taken anywhere and be given any task.

Thought for Reflection

When you dive into the deep waters, you will bear fruit every month of the year. You will catch multitudes of fish as you work hand in hand with other laid-down lovers. You will bring life and healing. You will know what to do and how to do it, as you remain immersed in the heart of God. Are you ready to hold up your part of the net?

Prayer

Lord, make me willing to work with those around me to bring people to You. Bring us all deep into intimacy with You so fruitfulness abounds and we can work together in joy and love.

DAY 26
HUNGER AND THIRST FOR GOD

Then Jesus said, "Truly, truly I say to you, Moses did not give you the bread from heaven, but My Father gives you the true bread from heaven. For the bread of God is He who comes down from heaven and gives life to the world." ... Jesus said to them, "I am the bread of life. Whoever comes to Me shall never hunger, and whoever believes in Me shall never thirst."
—JOHN 6:32–33, 35

Have you ever seen true hunger firsthand? Have you ever been to a third-world country, where the hungry are abundant? They always want something to eat. God is calling us to hunger and thirst after Him with the same desperation the poor have to find food. To learn about hunger, sit with the starving. To learn about thirst, sit with those who have nothing to drink.

The physical desperation among the poor often translates into spiritual hunger. Recently I was preaching to our Mozambican pastors at our Bible school in Pemba. Here are hungry and thirsty men, desperate for what is real. They are longing for God. But they are the poorest pastors I know, even though they are among the richest in the spirit realm. Days after discovering who Jesus is, they come to be trained to care for a group of others in the bush.

They often walk in with bare feet and ragged T-shirts. When we open the school, I ask how many of the pastors have had an immediate family member die of starvation. Often many hands are raised. We recently lost a pastor whose family was starving to death. In order to feed his family, he would dive into crocodile-infested rivers for water-lily bulbs. In trying to provide for his family, he was eaten alive.

We in the first, or Western, world often know very little about hunger. We find it difficult to even imagine having to do what this pastor did to feed his family. But we can learn from him. That's why I often have our Mozambican pastors come and pray for the westerners, in order to teach them about hunger. The pastors have certainly taught me.

Years ago, while I was learning about hunger, I had a vision of Jesus surrounded by a multitude of children. He looked at me with His intense, burning eyes of love, and I was completely undone. Jesus told me to feed the children, and I began to cry out loud, "No, there are too many!"

He asked me to look into His eyes, and He said, "I died so that there would always be enough."

Jesus has continually given us fresh bread from heaven. We live to be in His glorious presence. He has poured out His love to us without measure. He has called us to bring the lost children home. We are called to feed the hungry—both physically and spiritually.

Thought for Reflection

Spend time today reflecting on the desperation of those who hunger and thirst. Pray that you can begin to understand this desperation and that you will hunger and thirst with similar desperation for God. Then allow your condition to take you deeper into your relationship with Him.

Prayer

Lord, help me to understand what true hunger is, both physical hunger and spiritual hunger. Teach me what it means to be hungry for You. Help me to believe there will always be enough to satisfy me and those You call me to reach.

DAY 27
FEAST ON JESUS

But when you prepare a banquet, call the poor,
the maimed, the lame, the blind, and you will
be blessed, for they cannot repay you. You shall
be repaid at the resurrection of the just.
—LUKE 14:13–14

Have you ever been to a true feast, a feast
with food, a spirit of celebration, and joy?
The poor have taught me how to truly feast—
in both a physical and a spiritual sense.

One day some good friends gave us money
to buy chickens. Our children rarely eat
chicken, so they really know how to celebrate
during a feast. And no one would even listen
to my speaking because it was chicken time.

The kids were happy, and we invited every
bandit in town. Just as described in the parable in Luke, we went to gather all the poor,
the prostitutes, the drug addicts, and the
alcoholics, and we were making a ruckus. The

older mamas cooked the chicken one night for about seventeen hours, singing, "*Kamimanbu Xiquembu Shamatimba.*" (Thank you. God is great!)

After we finished preaching the message, the cook and a skeptical missionary believer asked me, "How many people did you invite today?" I told them, "Everyone we could find!" The Father invites us all to the great wedding feast in heaven, so on earth we like to do the same. We read God's mandate in Luke to invite them all—the poor, the crippled, the blind, the lame—and we did!

We told them to feed the visitors first, and they got a bit scared. They had counted 1,138 pieces of chicken—we knew that was a greasy job—but then they started thinking about all the people invited and thought, "We don't have enough." There were more than 2,200 people.

Often what we do is impossible in the natural, but we know that God can do anything! My theme and my theology is, "God is God. I am not. Hooray!"

So we all sat down to a chicken feast. Just as the passage in Luke 14 promises, all the bandits, drunkards, prostitutes, visitors, and children ate together. And there was more than enough!

There were even bags of chicken left over for the mamas to take home with them. It was a beautiful miracle confirmed by a very worried cook.

Watching those children devour greasy chicken helped to show me how to feast on Jesus. I want to partake of every part of Him. I want to hunger after Him, to delight in Him. I want to anticipate His communion with me. I want to thirst for His kingdom of righteousness to be established on the earth.

Thought for Reflection

The concept of feasting is an interesting one. It implies something much more than eating simply to satisfy hunger. It carries with it the idea of celebrating, of joyfully indulging in more food and drink—and perhaps more elaborate food and drink—than is usual. Considering this understanding of the term, how do you think it applies to your relationship with the Lord? How is it possible to "feast" on Him?

Prayer

Father, teach me how to feast. Let me learn from the hungry exactly how to feast on You. Help me to partake of every part of You and to delight in our fellowship.

Day 28
Eat and Drink of Me

As they were eating, Jesus took bread, blessed
it and broke it, and gave it to the disciples and
said, "Take and eat. This is My body." Then He
took the cup, and after He gave thanks, He gave
it to them, saying, "Drink of it, all of you. For
this is My blood of the new covenant, which
is shed for many for the remission of sins."
—MATTHEW 26:26–28

If you have ever been to a third-world country, or even to a poor neighborhood, you know how much the poor can teach you. For me, the poor taught me how to hunger for God and to take spiritual communion. Jesus invites us to eat and to drink of Him so that we become full. Just as we depend on food for our physical nourishment, we also need to depend on Jesus for the spiritual nourishment of our lives. We must feed on Him daily. Only then will we have the fresh bread from heaven that we need to give to both the spiritually and the naturally hungry.

Out of the abundance of our own feasting at His table, we will have fresh manna from heaven to give to the poor every day. As Mother Teresa once said:

> When Jesus came into the world, He loved it so much that He gave His life for it. He wanted to satisfy our hunger for God. And what did He do? He made Himself the Bread of Life. He became small, fragile, and defenseless for us. Bits of bread can be so small that even a baby can chew it. He became the Bread of Life to satisfy our hunger for God, our hunger for love.[1]

After we learn to eat of Him, we will then run into the darkness with fresh bread for the multitudes. For even the poor do not like stale bread. We cannot live on yesterday's manna or old revelation. Often in religious circles people are offered stale bread to eat, but no one wants it. So we must press into His presence and be filled with His real, fresh food every day or we will grow stale.

There is this fullness that Jesus promised: "Blessed are those who hunger and thirst for righteousness, for they shall be filled" (Matt. 5:6). The Father has invited all of us into His wedding feast to sit with Him, to come and eat. That means no more crumbs, no more stale bread, and no more garbage. We can just come in, let Him hold us, let Him love us, and let Him smile on us.

In Mozambique sometimes when we take the vulnerable children in, they run away and scavenge again in the dark places. But Jesus always leaves the ninety-nine to chase after the one. He always searches for the one lost coin. Jesus kills the fattened calf, throws the best party in town, and promises, "Son, you are always with me, and all that I have is yours" (Luke 15:31).

Thought for Reflection

The Lord promises in His Word that spiritual hunger will be filled. Let yourself hunger for Him, knowing He will fill you. Once He does, you can feed others—not dry, stale, tasteless bread but fresh manna from heaven.

Prayer

Lord, let me eat and drink my fill of You. Let me feast on You and share the fresh bread You give me with those who need Your love.

PART 4

REMAIN IN HIM

DAY 29
PRUNING

I am the true vine, and My Father is the vine-dresser. Every branch in Me that bears no fruit, He takes away. And every branch that bears fruit, He prunes, that it may bear more fruit. You are already clean through the word which I have spoken to you.
—JOHN 15:1–3

Have you ever pruned a tree or bush? Pruning involves cutting and removing dead or damaged parts from plants to increase their growth and fruitfulness.

Because God desires to increase our fruitfulness in the kingdom, He must prune us in a spiritual sense just as we would prune a plant. The process may seem painful to us at times because we do not understand exactly what is going on. But while He is pruning us above the ground, He is also multiplying our root system below. As He cuts off unyielding branches, our roots dig ever deeper.

Jesus is the true vine, and His Father is the gardener. Because the Father desires to see us flourish, He has to cut off every branch that bears no fruit. This hurts, but it comes from love. We would do well to take a posture before God that allows Him to prune anything and everything in us. Since we are called and chosen to be radical lovers who will carry the gospel to the ends of the earth, our destiny is to bear His glory, and His desire is to remove anything that hinders this goal.

Sometimes He chops off things we love. Sometimes He removes things we thought we liked. When He cuts off these branches and we start to feel the pain, He covers us with His kindness while continuing His work. His discipline always releases us into greater measures of our destiny.

God has delivered me from some things that used to bind me. He has cut away that which I used to think was there for a good reason. He looks gently at me, even though I may yell out in pain. He sees the end result and knows it is better than I can imagine.

If we do not understand His heart, passages such as John 15:1–2 might cause us to imagine God is mean. The God who holds a machete or pruning knife may not sound very cuddly—but the truth is that He is eternally gracious. He may chop and burn pieces of us, but when He does this, He will hold you in His arms and let you know He loves you.

After more than thirty-six years of missions I am starting to understand that every time He has chopped and burned anything in my life and the lives of those in our ministry, His work has brought more fruitfulness. Even if we have to change things that are very painful to change, we always say yes.

Thought for Reflection

Pruning is painful and hard. But God has a plan and knows what He is doing. Are you able to trust that He is pruning you so you may produce more fruit?

Prayer

Lord, pruning is hard. My initial reaction is to pull away and not allow it to happen. Help me to understand that pruning is for my good and to seek Your comfort and kindness in the process.

PRUNING THE GOOD FOR SOMETHING BETTER

Every branch in Me that bears no fruit, He takes away. And every branch that bears fruit, He prunes, that it may bear more fruit. You are already clean through the word which I have spoken to you. Remain in Me, as I also remain in you. As the branch cannot bear fruit by itself, unless it remains in the vine, neither can you, unless you remain in Me.
—JOHN 15:2–4

Have you ever had to choose between two good things and found yourself struggling to decide which was better? When God is pruning us, it can sometimes feel a little like that. Pruning is not always removing something dead or diseased; sometimes God decides to prune good areas of our lives—areas we love—because He wants something even better to grow there.

When God began to chop areas of my life,

He told me He was going to cut away, burn, and prune the things in my life that needed to go. I responded to God that there was one thing I would not negotiate.

Now it is not the smartest thing to tell God what you will and will not do. I do not suggest it to anyone. Even so, I told Him the one thing I always had to do was live with all the children. At that time we had hundreds of children living with us at our children's center. It was an incredibly loud place, and I had very little time to myself there, but I loved being close to all that was going on. I thrive on holy chaos.

At once I felt the Lord wooing and cutting away. He wanted to take me away and put me in a peaceful place instead. There was a home available to buy five minutes from our center, but I resisted. I had always lived in community among the people and all my children. I thought maybe the anointing would lift if I lived away from them.

But the Lord insisted. I felt His leading my husband and me to move away from our base into a house that was five minutes down the street. God was calling me to come away

with Him and spend more time in worship—
more time in the secret place.

As I invite His pruning, I can step out of
myself. It is what allows me to look into the
eyes of a hungry child or a dying grandmother
and realize there is truly always enough. I
agreed with the Lord that I would give Him
the most precious time in my day, no matter
how much the world and the church and the
people pressed in to take it away.

It is good to let Jesus cut away the branches
in us that do not bear fruit, but sometimes
even the branches that *do* bear fruit need
pruning so we can become even more fruitful. Living at the center was not a bad thing,
but God knew we could be more fruitful if
we had some time away.

God asks only that we trust Him. Abundant fruit is the result of surrender, and any
life that is laid down for the sake of love is a
ministry life.

Thought for Reflection

As God begins pruning you, keep in
mind that He has something better,
even if what He is removing seems to

be good. Surrender to Him throughout the process, and you will begin to see an abundance of fruit in your life. What aspect of your life or nature is He wanting to cut away today?

Prayer

Lord, help me to know that when You are pruning, You are doing it because You have something even better in mind. Help me to let go of those things You put Your finger on so Your plans for what is better can be fulfilled.

DAY 31
REMAIN IN HIM

Remain in Me, as I also remain in you. As the
branch cannot bear fruit by itself, unless it remains
in the vine, neither can you, unless you remain
in Me. I am the vine, you are the branches. He
who remains in Me, and I in him, bears much
fruit. For without Me you can do nothing.
—JOHN 15:4–5

As you fulfill the call God has placed on your life, it is important to make an effort to spend time with Him daily. You may have to put other things or people aside, but it is the only way to remain in Him and bear the fruit He requires of you.

When He asks me to take a long walk and worship Him, I gladly go. When He draws me into the ocean to look at the fish, I get my snorkel and dive in. I will go and worship underwater for hours if He calls me there. Some people might think I'm lazy by doing this, but I know more good fruit comes from this love affair than I could ever produce otherwise.

God wants your time at least as much as He wants mine! The Lord is asking you to give Him your time for the sake of love. What would it look like if we laid our precious cell phones and laptops on the altar before Him for even an hour or so each day?

When we hold to Him and remain in Him, our fruit will be sweet and wholesome and have no worms. Without Him, not a single grape can be found to give to the Father. He is the vine, and we are the branches. We can do absolutely nothing without Him. Nothing!

No is not always a popular word, but saying yes to God sometimes requires saying no to people who want things from us. We must be able to yield, not caring what it costs us to obey radically and love without limits. We must lay our lives on the altar and, for love's sake, obey.

Many people have had heavenly visitations or have received impressive-sounding prophetic words about being called to many nations, great ministries, or the media. But before all these things God asks us to make a covenant of obedience. Much of the time we do not need any new revelations, however powerful they may be. We need to abide in Him and obey the commands we have already been given. If we would do what we already know we are called to do, the world would be shaken to its core. This can and will happen as we remain in Him. To abide in His love is to obey Him.

God has called you to abide and remain in Him, the true vine, the source of all life. Who cares what it costs? *Of course* it will cost everything. You can expect that, but how much would you give for eternal love? Where would you go? What would you do?

Thought for Reflection

It may be not your mornings that you give to God, but your evenings. It may be your lunchtimes or your Saturdays. All of us are called to spend time alone with Him. Take the first step in obedience by committing to make fellowship with Him a priority.

Prayer

Here I am, Lord. Cut away everything You want to cut away. Burn off everything You want to burn off. Rearrange my schedule so that I can spend quality time in Your presence.

DAY 32
REMOVING THE
DEAD BRANCHES

*If a man does not remain in Me, he is thrown out
as a branch and withers. And they gather them
and throw them into the fire, and they are burned.*
—JOHN 15:6

Just as pruning is necessary for plants to have healthy growth, so God's pruning is necessary for us to grow spiritually and bear fruit. I admit that as a movement we are not always abiding as deeply as we could be, but together we are learning how to abide in the One who is altogether beautiful. We cannot write a neat, ten-step process for bearing fruit because we cannot create God's kind of fruitfulness. Perfect fruit comes from the perfect One. Our desire must be to enter His heart and love Him until fruit appears.

It is backward to try to love Him for the sake of fruit. Rather, we should desire fruit because we love Him. We are still learning more about this, but our goal is not to oversee some kind of world-leading, church-growth movement. Our one desire is to be in love with Him and to love Him well, and then to love every man, woman, and child we meet each day. All we really want is for our love to burn for Him, because we know that His love burns for us. He is for us. If we will yield, He will not let anything dead remain in us.

He says, "If a man does not remain in Me, he is thrown out as a branch and withers. And they gather them and throw them into the fire, and they are burned" (John 15:6). And so not only will He prune us, but He will also take every branch that does not bear fruit and burn it up. Everything that does not bring Him pleasure or that would lead to disobedience is going to be thrown into the fire. Before our eyes He is going to burn away anything that would hinder us. He is so in love with us that He will not allow dead branches to hang from our trees. His passion for us is too fierce and too jealous to let us squander our lives outside of connection to Himself, the true vine.

We each have dreams and destinies. I pray

God would burn away everything that does not bring Him pleasure—any desire that does not make His heart sing. I pray God would take us further into the secret place. When we do not know what to do or how to do it, I pray He would simply help us to yield more completely to Him. As He prunes us, He invites us into deeper intimacy. He invests Himself in our very dreams.

Thought for Reflection

Think about the words in today's Scripture verse. They are certainly not for the weak of heart. Jesus said, "If a man does not remain in Me, he is thrown out as a branch and withers"—and is eventually burned up. Yet He also promises that if we do abide in Him, we will bear much fruit. Which would you rather be—a branch that is discarded, or one that is connected to the Vine? Are you prepared to give God your permission to eliminate everything in your life that keeps you from Him?

Prayer

Lord, cut away anything in my life and in me that is not pleasing to You. Bearing fruit is more important than being comfortable. Help me to trust that You are doing what is good for me and for Your kingdom, even when it is painful.

DAY 33
ASK WHATEVER YOU DESIRE

If you remain in Me, and My words remain in
you, you will ask whatever you desire, and it shall
be done for you. My Father is glorified by this, that
you bear much fruit; so you will be My disciples.
—JOHN 15:7–8

Can you imagine a world in which God gives you whatever you desire? It is a world you can experience, one God wants all of us to experience.

How can this be? As we remain in Him, we get to know His heart more, and our desires become aligned with His. Jesus says, "If you remain in Me, and My words remain in you, you will ask whatever you desire, and it shall be done for you" (John 15:7).

What do you find yourself wanting when you abide in Him? This can be a perplexing question to ask, but I believe God trusts you. In this place He says we can ask of Him whatever we want. Do you want an unreached people group to know Jesus? Do you want a whole university to come to know His love? Do you want a cure for malaria?

I remember a time when I fell so deeply into the secret place that I sensed God was telling me to ask Him for anything I wanted. Some people think He should be telling us only what *He* wants. He does this too, but this time He was very definitely asking me what *I* wanted.

I told Him I wanted to see our movement care for a million children in my lifetime. I wanted to find all the children who were dying of starvation and bring them into a home. He liked that idea! I think maybe He even thought of it.

You see, when you spend time with Him in the secret place, a union takes place that causes you to start thinking like God. You begin to have His thoughts. You take on the mind of Christ. He finds it awesome that I want to care for a million children. I could have asked for a BMW—and I think I probably would have gotten one—but I wanted something else. In the secret place I had a mind connected with the presence and the purposes of God. I wanted children.

He wants to take you into that place too—where you have His mind and can ask for anything you want. When you are there, you will realize you must remain in Him for life.

Bearing good fruit demonstrates to the world that we are truly His disciples (John 15:8). A tree has to brave the wind, rain, and storm to release its fruit. It can be strong enough for this purpose only when it is deeply rooted in the soil. By remaining in Him, we allow Him to cultivate the soil beneath us. Each month as we rest in the river—careful to abide in obedience, spending time in the secret place—He promises to produce more and more good fruit through us.

He is your life source. He is the true vine. Without Him we can do nothing of any worth or lasting value, but He is glorified as we bear fruit from Him, with Him, and in Him.

Thought for Reflection

Our Father takes great pleasure when we release fruit that gives life to everyone around us. Give Him the time He asks for. Enter into His presence each day so that you can take on the mind of Christ and begin to think His thoughts, to have His desires. Then when you ask Him for anything, He will delight in filling your request.

Prayer

Jesus, let me be so close to You that Your desires become My desires. I want to want what You want and to see Your perfect will fulfilled on the earth.

DAY 34
THE COST OF OBEDIENCE

By this we know the love of God: that He laid down His life for us, and we ought to lay down our lives for the brothers. Whoever has the world's goods and sees his brother in need, but closes his heart of compassion from him, how can the love of God remain in him?
—1 JOHN 3:16–17

Have you ever asked your mother what it was like to be pregnant with you? Chances are it wasn't the easiest time in her life. Expectant mothers often feel stretched and pulled. Going through the discomfort of carrying the baby's extra weight is part of the process. Even when circumstances are good, it is not easy. There are nights when mothers cannot sleep and days when they cannot eat. There is the pain of birth. But all turns to joy when the baby arrives!

The same can be true when God wants to

move spiritually through us. One time, at a church conference in Red Deer, Canada, the Lord overshadowed me. I was crying out, "Take me and use me! Bruise me, if need be." Suddenly I felt as if I was being pulled inside the Lord's heart. I heard His next words clearly: "Go and get my lost Makua bride." I did not know the first thing about who the Makua were, but immediately my heart was broken for them.

After some research my husband informed me the Makua were the most unreached tribal group in southeast Africa. Millions of Makua people happened to live in the far north of Mozambique. I realized that to reach them, we would have to leave the southern part of the country. I began to feel the weight and pain of what God had asked us to do. We would have to leave behind most of the children at our southern base. We loved them dearly.

It took us awhile to get ready and train our southern team, who would continue the base there, but after about one year we moved to the town of Pemba in northern Mozambique. At that time we had no northern base, no buildings, and nowhere permanent to live. I found myself once again sharing the gospel on street corners.

The cost of moving was high, but who can put a price on obeying the Lord?

Most of the greatest miracles Rolland and I have ever witnessed occurred during our most difficult personal trials. When our circumstances were the most stressful, food started multiplying. The blind started to see. The deaf started to hear. Some of our pastors saw people raised from the dead.

Sometimes life is tough, and obeying the Lord in these tough times is difficult. Persevere regardless. Say yes regardless. You never know what God wants to birth in these uncomfortable times.

Thought for Reflection

Are you one who will carry God's promise? Do you burn with His heart for the lost? Will you say yes, even when stretched and pulled, inconvenienced, and made uncomfortable? Will carry His love—whether to those who are obviously poor, naked, wretched, and blind, or to those who think they are rich but are lacking in faith? Will you go and get His lost bride wherever He sends you?

Prayer

Lord, when life gets uncomfortable and You are calling me out of my comfort zone to do Your work, help me to be strong and willing to pay the price. Remind me of the fruit You are bringing forth so that I will remain steadfast.

Day 35
Giving It All Up for the Kingdom

Then Jesus, looking upon him, loved him and said to him, "You lack one thing: Go your way, sell whatever you have and give to the poor, and you will have treasure in heaven. And come, take up the cross and follow Me."
—MARK 10:21

If God asked you to give away all that you have to those who need it, how would you respond? Would you hesitate? Would you wonder how you would survive without your possessions? God will honor us for joyfully giving what He asks of us, even when we don't understand.

One of my heroes is Pastor José from Maputo. We co-pastored our Zimpeto church together for many years. Today Pastor José is a leader over thousands of churches. A few years back I watched him as he once lay facedown in the dirt in our church; he was sobbing. Saint Simeon once said that tears are a sign of the Holy Spirit's presence. I watched as this man wept puddles of tears on that dirty concrete floor.

Finally I asked Pastor José why he was crying. His reply to me was, "I am very full of joy. God just told me to give away everything I have."

I was thinking, "You don't have anything. You live in a tin hut." And I knew that rats would come into his house at night and chew on things—even his and his wife's toes—but I never heard either of them complain. At the moment that I saw him sobbing in the dirt, I knew I could trust him. Now he serves as one of the international directors of Iris Ministries.

Three days later my construction contractor told me that Pastor José had taken every single thing he owned and given it to the poor. This man walked in the true authority that comes only from meekness and being trustworthy to God. He had a humble heart.

An Australian team came to help, but they knew nothing of what was going on. They just watched Pastor José sob before God and walk miles each day to work to love the poor and the children. The team told him, "We'll build you a new house." Guess what Pastor José did? He filled his new house with children who had been abandoned or orphaned and made them sons.

When you seek first the riches of heaven, God also entrusts you with those on earth.

Soon after that team had built him the house, another person gave Pastor José a well. Now he had water for all those children whom he had adopted as his own. He was then given electricity so he could have lights. Pastor José did not know what to do with all this! If you live a life of humility, then God will trust you with much.

Thought for Reflection

Are you willing to give up all that you have if God calls you to? What about leaving behind your home to share His love with those in another part of the world? Not everyone is called to be a missionary, but each one of us must be willing to surrender all to serve Him.

Is there anything you would withhold from Him?

Prayer

Lord, prepare me to do whatever You ask of me. Help me to surrender all I have and all I am to You before You even ask. Help me to always say yes.

Following Fearlessly

There is no fear in love, but perfect love casts out fear, because fear has to do with punishment. Whoever fears is not perfect in love.
—1 JOHN 4:18

Have you ever questioned whether you should take the next step in the ministry God has called you to? Most believers have. Fear of failure, the unknown, or even God's asking them to do something they don't feel equipped to do holds many Christians back. In truth some experience real danger when they obey God's call. But the Bible tells us we are not to be afraid. "Perfect love casts out fear" (1 John 4:18).

We have certainly had our share of dangerous situations. People have shot at us, thrown us in jail, and kicked us out of our homes. I have been shipwrecked, beaten, carjacked, stoned, and threatened with knives and guns. In fact, I can no longer count the number of times my life has been threatened. When it happens now, I often laugh. Being in love with God brings a fearlessness that surpasses understanding. He is worth it all!

Once in Mozambique I was walking down the street. Without warning a truckload of police raced up the street and pulled up in front of us. Eight men with assault rifles pointed them at my head. They told me to get in the truck. They were going to take me to jail because I had recently been preaching in the prisons without permission.

I laughed at them and refused to get in the truck. I told them I would walk with them alongside their truck to go to jail. Once there they put me in a room, but then the police chief who really wanted me in jail was called away for an emergency, so the police let me go but told me I had to come back the next day at eight in the morning.

I felt like the Holy Spirit told me to go in at eight o'clock sharp. I did not know the reason why, but I obeyed. It turns out the chief had just left on emergency business when I was there for a second time.

I asked the ranking policeman what his name was. He told me, and it was a biblical name. I shared about this policeman's namesake and prayed for Him to meet Jesus, and at once the Holy Spirit fell on him. Not only did the policeman let me go, but he also spoke to his police chief on our behalf. That month Iris Global received an official letter allowing us to minister in all the jails and prisons in that province.

What could they do? What can anyone do when you are fearless? When you cannot be made to fit into preconceived boxes, even people who want to think of you as an enemy will not know what to do with you. But you can be truly fearless only when you are in love—when you are immersed and yielded to the point that you do not care about the cost.

The world will not understand. They don't know what to do with the kind of fearlessness that comes from being drowned in His love. You will need this courage. When God puts a dream inside your heart, you can expect that it will cost you something. The destiny He wants to release through your life is no light matter. Seek this vision fearlessly. It is the most joyful thing you can ever do, but it is also a sacred mandate to practice sacrificial love.

Thought for Reflection

When you are in love with God and ready to pay any price to serve Him, you won't be afraid of what the world can do to you. You will know that your life is not your own—to use or to lose. God is in charge, and His purposes will prevail.

Prayer

Lord, I know times ahead may be rough and I may be tempted to give in to fear. Help me to walk fearlessly, trusting You, as I move forward in what You are calling me to do.

Day 37
Blessed Are the Merciful

Blessed are the merciful, for they shall obtain mercy.
—MATTHEW 5:7

Have you ever been asked to forgive someone? What if this person hurt you deeply? What if he hurt one of your children? Mercy is difficult to dole out, but it is essential for us to extend it to those who harm us if we want to be like Jesus.

One of my favorite stories about God and His mercy involves a man named Horacio. A few years ago we had a regional conference. Our conferences are a little different from Western conferences. All our people sleep outside in the dirt or on the floor of the church.

At about 4:00 p.m. Horacio went outside to lock the gate and to quiet a gang that had come there to cause trouble. But the gang jumped on him and beat him severely until he died. At 12:15 a.m., while the church was gathered together praying in one accord, Horacio came back to life! His whole face and body were swollen, his clothes were shredded, and he was in excruciating pain. The doctors did not know what to do except to give him morphine for the pain. Before he went to sleep from the medicine, through his broken and swollen lips he said just two words: "Forgive them."

The church kept praying and considering what should be done with the gang if the police caught them. Before long it was agreed that according to what Horacio had said, the church would forgive them. Later in the morning the police caught one of the gang members. They called the church and asked that someone come and file charges at the police station. A pastor told them there was a little problem because the man who had been murdered was no longer dead, and the church decided that no charges would be filed against the gang. The pastor and the church were firm. They believed that mercy triumphs over justice and forgiveness always wins. So the boy was forgiven and released into the church's custody.

As soon as the decision was made to forgive the young man, Horacio's body was totally healed. He was totally well; he had no swelling, bruising, scars, or problems whatsoever. It was as though he had never been attacked the night before. The only evidence left from the attack was his clothes. Someone had to go out and buy new clothes for him because his others were torn to shreds from the beating. The next morning Horacio himself went to the police station to pick up the teenager. The police were still very angry and said, "Do whatever you want with him."

Remembering Matthew 5:7—"Blessed are the merciful, for they shall obtain mercy"—the entire community decided to respond in a spirit opposite to the one that had motivated the gang, and they ministered to the teen with deep love and compassion. Within an hour the boy gave his heart to Jesus.

Thought for Reflection

Mercy is difficult to give and rarely deserved, but God can work mightily through us when we extend it to others. Think of what Jesus suffered to obtain mercy for you, and it will come more easily.

Prayer

Lord, help me to be merciful, as You are. I know You can work in powerful ways when I extend mercy and forgiveness to those who hurt me. Teach me to care more about extending Your kingdom than about demanding justice for offenders.

DAY 38
THOSE WHO ARE FORGIVEN MUCH LOVE MUCH

Therefore I say to you, her sins, which are
many, are forgiven, for she loved much. But
he who is forgiven little loves little.
—LUKE 7:47

Extending mercy to those we feel don't deserve it is difficult—God has to work in us to make it possible. I learned this lesson from a young girl named Orpa, who taught me about the blessing of extending mercy and living a life embodying the Beatitudes.

One day we were in Maputo, just sitting on the street, when suddenly I heard gunshots. The police were shooting at and trying to kill some kids who had been stealing. I did my best to protect one of the boys. Meanwhile, at a distance, a disabled girl named Orpa watched me as I held this boy in my arms. She tried to hide the tears that were rolling down her cheeks until she hobbled over to where I sat with him.

I asked her if she would like to talk. I asked the girl what had happened to her. She told me she had been burned in a fire. Since she was permanently disabled, her family thought she would no longer be of any use. Her family decided that her brothers would kill her. The brothers took her to a field, threw rocks at her, and left her there to die.

Orpa said she was filled with anger. She would scream and roll on the ground. She wanted to see her family dead. But God sent a man who, like the good Samaritan, saw her in the field, stopped to help her, and took her to a hospital, and she stayed there for nine months.

When she was released, she was forced to sell her body for food to eat. Was this justice? It was not the love of God. How could this happen?

After a little while I was able to speak to Orpa about a man who would look at her with pure eyes. I told her that this man would think she was beautiful—that man is Christ Jesus, who gave up His life for her. Orpa received

Jesus right there in the streets before she came home to live with us at our children's center.

At first Orpa still talked about how she hated her family for trying to kill her. But as she grew in love with Jesus, she also grew in mercy. The love of God flowing through that girl just amazed me. After a few months she came to me and told me she wanted to go home. She wanted to go and tell her brothers about Jesus, and she wanted her other family members to meet Him too. When you know you are truly forgiven, you learn how to forgive. Orpa, who had been full of hatred and anger, received God's mercy and forgiveness. Even if her family killed her when she went back home, she was determined to show mercy to them and let the light of Jesus shine.

Thought for Reflection

Forgiving those who have hurt you is necessary for moving forward in your relationship with God and seeing the miraculous birthed in your life. Does the example of Orpa motivate you to forgive more readily?

Prayer

Lord, let me never forget that You paid a debt for me so that the Father would have mercy on me and forgive me of my sins. Cause this realization to motivate me to always extend mercy to others, no matter what I suffer at their hands.

DAY 39
BLESSED ARE THOSE WHO ARE PERSECUTED

Blessed are those who are persecuted for righteousness' sake, for theirs is the kingdom of heaven.
—MATTHEW 5:10

In the first world, a world of prosperity and plenty, it seems paradoxical for a person to be "blessed"—that is, spiritually prosperous or joyful—when experiencing persecution. But regardless of the outward situation, Christ in us can be our hope of glory, our joy unspeakable (Col. 1:27).

In the first-world church, there is often an escapist mentality. We shrink away from persecution. Certainly there is no inherent value in persecution for its own sake, but we can experience a blessing through it. When we persevere through the suffering, knowing that Jesus can identify with our pain and bring good out of it, and pray for our persecutors to come into a saving knowledge of Him, we can truly be a blessed people no matter the circumstance.

Jesus knew persecution like no other: "He was despised and rejected of men, a man of sorrows and acquainted with grief…he was despised, and we did not esteem him. Surely he has borne our grief and carried our sorrows" (Isa. 53:3–4). Jesus was misunderstood by all, even His own parents—"He came to His own, and His own people did not receive Him" (John 1:11). He nevertheless demonstrated love to those who rejected Him again and again.

We sometimes imagine persecution only through the lens of physical suffering: being beaten, stoned, jailed, and suffering for His name's sake. But there is a greater pain that comes from being rejected by those you love. Jesus poured forth limitless, ceaseless, bottomless love to each and every person in front of Him, regardless of the pain. Because He has known the worst pain, Jesus can relate to anything we are going through. "For we do not have a High Priest who cannot sympathize with our weaknesses, but

One who was in every sense tempted like we are" (Heb. 4:15).

Thought for Reflection

Persecution is something most westerners have difficulty understanding. However, it is possible for a person to be blessed even in the midst of persecution. Do you see how this could be the case? When you are made to suffer for Christ, trust in Him. He understands your pain and will uphold you in the midst of it.

Prayer

Father, help me to understand how You can bring forth good from persecution. Help me to see Your blessings regardless of the circumstances surrounding me.

Day 40
Love in the Midst
of Persecution

*Do not be grieved, for the joy of
the LORD is your strength.*
—NEHEMIAH 8:10

It can be difficult to show kindness when someone is treating you unfairly. Our natural instinct is to lash out in anger or fear. But God can work miracles in situations in which we act in a spirit opposite to that of our oppressors.

God sent me to Mexico City with a team from Vanguard University of Southern California to minister to the poor. We were doing street theater among the poor when suddenly our team was grabbed by the police. They screamed and yelled at us, but God spoke to me about not reacting to my persecutors. Still, they threw us in jail.

We began to worship and thank God. Our church hosts were fasting and praying for us.

We knew God was with us, but the police continued to abuse and ridicule us verbally. And then, suddenly everything changed.

One of my friends, who is six feet four inches tall, began to walk on his hands. Seeing this giant man clowning around took them off guard. They all began to laugh. Soon after, the guards, who were now amused, decided to release us.

If your reaction is meekness and kindness, then you will be blessed even if you don't feel blessed. If we had yelled or pushed back at the police, we would have lost the opportunity to choose love. We will always ask Jesus how to represent Him in each and every circumstance. In that jail cell in Mexico City I learned to let the joy of the Lord be my strength. When we choose joy—not retribution—the kingdom of God breaks forth in the most unlikely circumstances.

Love never fails. Choosing to react in love to persecution is perhaps the godly love described in 1 Corinthians 13: "Love suffers long and is kind; love envies not; love flaunts not itself and is not puffed up, does not behave itself improperly, seeks not its own, is not easily provoked, thinks no evil; rejoices not in iniquity, but rejoices in the truth; bears all things, believes all things, hopes all things, and endures all things" (vv. 4–8).

Thought for Reflection

Are you able to choose joy over revenge or anger or hatred? Do you trust yourself to choose to love even in the most difficult circumstances? You cannot do it out of your own strength; you must allow the Holy Spirit to shed abroad the love of God in and through you.

Prayer

Lord, I want to honor You in the midst of persecution and unfairness. Help me to love and to show joy in times of trial. Teach me to lean on You to help me through.

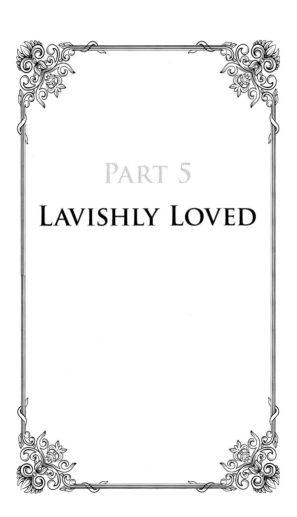

PART 5

LAVISHLY LOVED

Day 41
Lavishly Loved

Consider how much love the Father has given to
us, that we should be called children of God.
—1 JOHN 3:1

You are a son or daughter of God. He loves you deeply, in a way words cannot describe.

Understanding that you are a son or a daughter of God and that the Father lavishly loves you is what makes you free to enter your destiny. Only this understanding can give you confidence enough to say yes to the fullness of the call God will put in your heart. If you can catch even a glimpse of how warmly God smiles on you, you will want to give Him everything for the rest of your life. You will go to the ends of the earth for Him. Whether it means living in the dirt with the poorest of the poor or being salt and light to Harvard elites, we are all called to shine in our own way. God has a special pair of shoes just for you, perfectly suited for your own path. You must learn to wear your own shoes and never put on anyone else's. Walk in your anointing.

Lavish is an incredibly rich word. It means "over the top, more than you could imagine"— as when we read, "Consider how much love the Father has given to us, that we should be called children of God" (1 John 3:1).

No matter how great we are, we do not naturally deserve to be called sons and daughters of God. Even if we achieved top academic honors in school, the highest promotions at our jobs, and every other qualification this world could possibly offer, we would never merit such a gift. Only His free and lavish love gives us the most beautiful title of all—not doctor, not lawyer, not apostle, but son or daughter.

We are the family God went out and found. He was so determined to call us sons and daughters that He suffered on a cross and died. Jesus and His Father are one. Whatever Jesus does, the Father does. They act together, and the cross expresses the unity of their love for us. Jesus died so we could be brothers and sisters to one another. Before that we could not be one family.

I have been beaten up, shot at, and lied about. People have even tried to strangle me. I am not afraid. To this day I can walk boldly into gangs of armed thugs and tell them to stop in the name of Jesus. I expect them to drop their knives. Generally they turn surprisingly nice. Sometimes they look at me and apologize.

Where did this confidence come from? It came from knowing the Father loves me. Because I truly know that I am loved, I am not afraid.

God wants your ministry to flow from the realization that you are a beloved child of God. In that place you don't worry too much about how people see you. You don't worry too much about whether they're nice or mean. You don't even worry about whether they love you or hate you. You don't worry because you're simply going to love them and love Him. Your confidence comes from knowing who He is and what He thinks of you. This is what it means to grasp that you are a child of God.

Thought for Reflection

Do you understand just how loved you are? How would knowing and accepting that truth change you, your actions, and your fulfillment of God's calling on your life?

Prayer

Jesus, help me to grasp the reality of Your infinite and unconditional love for me. Help me to revel in the knowledge of this love. Let it shape how I live and how I minister to others.

DAY 42
LOVED WHILE
STILL SINNERS

*But God, being rich in mercy, because of His
great love with which He loved us, even when
we were dead in sins, made us alive together
with Christ (by grace you have been saved).*
—EPHESIANS 2:4–5

What if we make messy mistakes? What
if it turns out we are still flawed people who
can be difficult to get along with? Will He
keep on loving us then?

We have taken in thousands of children to
live with us over the years. One of them was
a particular rascal. If he could find something
wrong to do, he would do it. He stole everything he could get his hands on. He beat up
his brothers and sisters. He was a compul-
sive liar. He was angry, bitter, and incredibly
inventive in finding new ways to be difficult.

I asked God what to do about this one.

God told me to love him. I responded that I *did* love him. Frustrated, I asked the Lord *how* He wanted me to love him. I sensed the Lord saying He wanted me to give him some time and to pray for him every day and that then God would bring him into His own house. So that is what I and the other caretakers did. For a long time we could see no progress. After a while he managed to move out of the country.

Recently, when I was speaking, I saw this spiritual son again. At once I was startled to see how powerfully the presence of God was resting on him. When he came up to me, he started weeping and shaking in my arms. In broken English he said, "Thank you, Mama, for not stop loving me."

While we embraced, suddenly I felt God ask me if I would have given my life for this one.

"*Yes*," I responded. "*I would have given my life for this one.*"

When Jesus gave Himself for us, He was looking forward to the joy set before Him. (See Hebrews 12:2.) Our joy in this son was seeing him filled with the presence of God. Our joy was seeing him come home to the

Father's house and step into the spirit of adoption.

That boy—now a man—knows now who he is. He is a son. He knows better than most that God loves him no matter what he has done. He is loved because of the incredible grace of God that comes down to call each of us sons and daughters. None of us deserve it. We simply have it.

Your heavenly Father loves you in the same way, no matter what you do or how you fail. This is the love He spoke over us when He sent His Son. It is what Jesus poured out on the cross. Because of this love we have become children of God.

Thought for Reflection

You are a son or a daughter of God right now—today. Your real identity is in this truth. It doesn't matter what people do or do not call you. It doesn't matter what you have done. You are a son. You are a daughter. Believe it! How does this identity impact the way you see yourself?

Prayer

Lord, help me to believe that You love me with the love of a father—in spite of my flaws and my mistakes. Help me to lay hold of the truth that You would have died on the cross to secure my redemption, even if I were the only person in the world.

DAY 43
THE SPIRIT OF ADOPTION

He chose us in Him before the foundation of the world, to be holy and blameless before Him in love.
—HEBREWS 1:4

Have you ever watched children in a new environment? If they feel as if they don't belong, it is obvious. An orphaned and abandoned spirit causes people to shrink back, peer around corners, and not believe that there is room enough for them on their Father God's lap. This is true for the children we rescue from terrible circumstances, but, more surprisingly, it is true for all of us.

When we first take in children from the street, they are usually little bandits whose bodies are full of lice and scabies, and they are generally really rotten rascals. They are not nice, sweet little children! They are not cuddly little angels. But we welcome them with open arms into our villages.

On the weekends we have sleepovers with children who live in our center. Some have lived there a long time, while others are brand-new additions to our Iris family. At first the new ones are so timid that they won't even eat anything from the fridge. They feel that they have to work for what they want—or steal it. The children who know who they are with us open the fridge and help themselves to everything!

The new children do not yet understand that they were chosen before the foundation of the world; they were predestined to be God's children. They do not yet understand His grace or know that they were adopted as sons through Jesus Christ in accordance with His pleasure and will (Eph. 1). They are still afraid, and they often steal or think they must earn everything and strive for acceptance. They have to learn about adoption into God's family and then trust that they really are wanted. It is a delight to see when they really have a true experience of adoption. They truly do change and find joy! This can happen only as a gift of the Holy Spirit.

The spirit of adoption means we were

hand-chosen by our heavenly Father. With that choosing comes our rights as sons and daughters of our Father. Let me offer you an illustration. I have two children. I did not get to pick them; I gave birth to them. But I think they are absolutely awesome. I never say, "Hey, I wish you were more like…" No, they are flesh of my flesh and truly amazing people. They make my heart sing. But when we adopt children, we actually go out and look for them—we choose them.

After over twenty years of ministering to children in the streets and villages of Mozambique, I am beginning to understand more about the spirit of adoption. God is looking for spiritual fathers and mothers who know who they are in Him, who will go into the darkness, look for the spiritually lost of all ages, and bring them home to the Father's house.

Our attempts to minister to others may be feeble to some, but they are precious to God. We may minister like a three-year-old drawing her first picture, but we try as hard as we can, and with great joy we scribble our picture for God. We may mess it up or rip the page. But when God our Father looks at what we have done for Him, He says, "It's amazing; it's fabulous!" If God had a fridge in heaven, our pictures would be on it.

Thought for Reflection

Just as it takes time for the children in Mozambique to understand after being adopted that they are a part of the family, it can take us some time to truly understand that we are a part of God's family. Rest in the fact that He chose you. He wants you to be His, and He is calling you to work with Him.

Prayer

Lord, thank You for choosing me to be one of Your children. Help me to accept Your love and to be delivered from an orphaned and abandoned spirit once and for all.

DAY 44
FROM SPIRITUAL
ORPHAN TO HEIR

*He said to him, "Son, you are always with
me, and all that I have is yours."*
—LUKE 15:31

Do you live as if you are an heir of God? This
is a big transformation and an important one.
It is a spiritual transformation we see mirrored
in the children we adopt in Mozambique.

Endrik is another one of our Mozambican
children. When he first came to us, he would
run around and bite and kick people, looking miserable all the time. Endrik had experienced great pain in his early childhood and
had never known love. Both of his parents
had died. There was so much shame and sadness in him that he would not look anyone in
the eye. Endrik did not think he had access
to Rolland, to me, or to our family.

Like some of the other children, Endrik

could not comprehend what a fridge was because he had never seen one before. He would not dare to go toward the fridge, and he had never had a Coca-Cola in his life. So I took Endrik by the hand and told him, "That fridge has a Coke in it. You can go get that Coke whenever you want it." I also said, "Endrik, I'm going to tuck you in and sing you a song. I will look you in the eyes, and I will love you."

Then God started transforming his little heart.

We are all a bit like this with God. We think things like, "Am I really allowed? Can I really open that door and drink of Him? Does He really love me?" But over time God heals our abandoned and orphaned spirits.

Finally one day Endrik walked up to that fridge and took the drink. The first time he opened the fridge door and realized that he belonged to the family, joy hit his heart and spiked across his face. He realized that he had full access to the house.

All that is in God's house is available to His sons and daughters too. We are allowed to partake of His peace, His joy, His patience, His long-suffering, His healing, and His provision. We are free to be intimate with Him and walk into the secret place as a son or daughter.

Many of us are like Endrik. Although we have access to the heavenly realm, we are not sure whether the Father wants to see us. Some wonder whether there is a God who is near or if He actually hears us. Others think that God does hear them but that He does not want to answer them. First John 4:18 tells us, "There is no fear in love. But perfect love drives out fear, because fear has to do with punishment. The one who fears is not made perfect in love."

Most of us stand at the fridge door, wondering if God is going to slap our hands if we dare to open it and feast in the Father's house. Or we think that God is low on Cokes and wants to save them for the special children—or at least save them for some other time when we are really good. So we timidly step away from God. This is the abandoned and orphaned spirit.

Such vulnerable children compete with each other, always comparing and worrying that there is not enough, worrying that if God blesses someone else, they will miss out. Sons and daughters of God who are pure in heart give preference to each other, knowing that there is always enough in the Father's house.

Thought for Reflection

When God welcomes you home, exchanging your abandoned and orphaned spirit for a spirit of sonship, you can boldly come forward, realizing that a loving Father declares, "All that I have is yours" (Luke 15:31). Are you eager to partake of all He has to offer you? Are you ready to live as an heir rather than an outcast?

Prayer

Lord, I believe You have made me Yours. Help me to live in this truth by moving and acting without hesitation as a child of God. Teach me to come to You in confidence, knowing You love me and desire fellowship with me.

DAY 45
EQUALLY YOKED IN LOVE

And I heard a loud voice from heaven, say-
ing, "Look! The tabernacle of God is with men,
and He will dwell with them. They shall be His
people, and God Himself will be with them and
be their God. 'God shall wipe away all tears from
their eyes. There shall be no more death.' Nei-
ther shall there be any more sorrow nor crying nor
pain, for the former things have passed away."
—REVELATION 21:3–4

The idea of being equally yoked is common among Christians. But have you ever thought about how it applies to us and God instead of to a married couple? If we are to be yoked with God, we have to be equally yoked in the sense that we love as He loves.

To become a bride equally yoked in love, we follow the footsteps of Jesus. We must, in love, empty ourselves and become poor in spirit to gain the riches of heaven and be filled with Him. Jesus gave all for His bride when He came to dwell among us. Now we give up our lives to be married to Him and inherit the riches of heaven.

The Christian life is all about union and communion. As Revelation 21 describes, God has chosen to make His dwelling with us, to call us His people. In Jesus, our servant King, God has united Himself with humanity. In union with Jesus, we inherit a new heaven and a new earth. When two people are truly in love, they will each give all that they have for the other. God does not want us to merely love as Jesus does. His desire is to possess our very nature with *His* love.

This bride will be radiant and dazzling, altogether lovely like her Bridegroom King. She will have the same Spirit, being like-minded, doing nothing out of selfish ambition or vain conceit. She will consider others more than herself. She will be led by Philippians 2, which says, "Let nothing be done out of strife or conceit, but in humility let each esteem the other better than himself. Let each of you look not only to your own interests, but also the interests of others" (vv. 3–4).

This bride will give up the selfish riches of this world to inherit the earth. She will be so ruined and wrecked by love that she will run full force into the darkness. This will cause His light through her to explode into the world—all for love's sake.

We must give our life, in marriage, to another—to our Bridegroom, King Jesus. If we embrace the Sermon on the Mount, our life no longer is our own, and yet it is the most fulfilling, exciting, and joyful life imaginable. God knows how to bless us with the true riches of heaven.

Thought for Reflection

Becoming like Jesus is both necessary and inevitable as we are yoked with Him. Allow this process to happen. Today, give up selfish desires and your own ambitions; He has something better for you.

Prayer

Lord, help me to become more and more like You. I give myself to You now. Let Your love shape me into a new creation that resembles You.

DAY 46
LOVING AS JESUS DID

Beloved, now are we children of God, and it has not yet been revealed what we shall be. But we know that when He appears, we shall be like Him, for we shall see Him as He is.
—1 JOHN 3:2

Do you want to be like Jesus? Do you want to look like Him, smell like Him, and feel like Him? I do! I may have a long way to go, but that is my only goal. I want to act like Him and love as He does.

The apostle John tells us that when Christ appears, we will be like Him (1 John 3:2). Every single one of us is created in His image. Even those we seem least able to understand are made in the image of God. Each one has intrinsic value. Each carries divine beauty.

We need to look at people the way Jesus does. He gave Himself so that all would know His lavish love. To show this love is our call. It is the one goal for which we have many different anointings.

This call is not something too difficult for us to understand. We cannot run from it. Our task is to love everyone around us until each one knows what it means to be a child of the living God. We must serve one another until we have all grasped the spirit of adoption. We must see the beauty we bear.

Because we are His sons and daughters, He has promised us He will not leave us fatherless (John 14:18). God is faithful to His Word—no one is to remain fatherless. If we are to be like Him and love as He does, part of our work must be making sure no one remains orphaned or abandoned. Sometimes when visitors come, we can tell they were expecting to see a lot of misery. They show up and seem surprised that our children are happy. We tell them this is because they have been adopted. They have family. They are full of love.

We spend a lot of time hugging the children. We pray God's love over them constantly. We do our best to love them as Jesus loves them, and the spirit of adoption overwhelms them. Personally I have never seen happier children anywhere else.

Sometimes people pity us. They say, "You work with the poor. There is malaria, cholera, dysentery. You hang out in the slums. You make such great sacrifices!" We laugh. None of this seems like any great sacrifice to us. We are glad to give our lives and to obey the call of God by loving as Jesus did. We are ministers who are filled up with the joy of the Lord; this is our strength.

He asks you to give love as freely as you have received it—not just to those who deserve it but also to everyone He puts in front of you.

Thought for Reflection

Loving as Jesus loves means loving people until they receive the spirit of adoption. It means loving them until they accept that they are children of God. Are you able to love this way?

Prayer

Lord, I want to be like You, and that means loving as You do. Help me to *love—and keep on loving—those You put in front of me until they believe they are part of Your family.*

Day 47
Comforting Those Who Mourn

Blessed are those who mourn, for they shall be comforted.
—MATTHEW 5:4

Mourning is all too often a part of this life. It is something we have become too familiar with at our home in Mozambique. In one week's time, eight of our precious little ones died. I found myself in a state of exhaustion. I didn't understand. I loved them so much. I couldn't help but wonder why. They just seemed to die one after another. The only thing I could do was ask Jesus, "What do I do? What do we do?"

Jesus replied, "Either way, you win because you loved them to life." I got a picture of His arms opening wide to receive those babies. My incredible mourning found a place of comfort in knowing that we had rescued these children from places of despair and loneliness. We knew that we had shown them God's love.

Many, many questions began to arise: How do we become the hands and feet of Jesus to dying humanity? How do we bring comfort? How do we become the love of Jesus in a culture that is crying? How do we become the kindness—the mercy—of Jesus in a culture that is mourning? And, more specifically, how do *you* become a blessing for the poor? It must be incarnational love!

Every culture has a common denominator of misery and pain. From Korea to Mozambique, and then to Brazil and America, every society has a felt need that we must identify and offer to meet in order to comfort them. A minister's job is not simply to preach on a platform, standing up in front of a crowd of people while a big film crew records the service. This is not our primary purpose. Our job is to love each person, one at a time, to stop and lend help every day for each of the suffering and the sick.

Some say, "Can we love without money?" The answer is yes. And the simplest way to demonstrate love is to hold someone in your arms, to look them in the eyes, and to offer them a smile. How do you become good news to both the poor and the rich? How do you become love manifested in physical form and see this gospel fulfilled? If you are called as a missionary—a "sent-out one"—then you are called to comfort those who mourn. You are called to love the broken until they understand God's love—a love that never dies—through you.

Yes, God wants you to do signs and wonders. But the love of God manifested through you is what people really need. So you must first see His face. You must become so close to His very heartbeat that you can feel what others feel. I want to live as if I am hidden in His very heart, where His thoughts become my thoughts and His ways become my ways. This is how we will reach the world.

Thought for Reflection

Sometimes people need to see signs and wonders, but more often they just need to feel God's love for them. God can use you to show this love. Pray that you can feel as others feel. As your heart breaks with theirs, God's love can shine through.

Prayer

Lord, show me how to comfort those who are mourning and suffering. Teach me to discern what they need, whether it is for You to simply love them through me or for You to manifest Your power in a miraculous way.

DAY 48
THE LEAST OF THESE

Truly I say to you, as you have done it for one of the least of these brothers of Mine, you have done it for me.
—MATTHEW 25:40

Some of you already know you are called to be a missionary. Others of you may still want to know your callings. Let this be your call: Comfort a sad woman. Comfort a mourning child. Comfort a dying man.

Most of my heroes are from third-world nations. I remember the day when a four- or five-year-old child named Camila who had been badly raped was left abandoned. I was not doing some crusade or apostolic, history-making thing. I simply looked down on this emaciated child and thought, "God, this is what I am created for. I am created to stop for this one." This is where I was to give comfort.

All the sweet girl did was cry. I wondered,

"What does it look like to be Jesus to this person, to a people group, or to this nation?"

Matthew 5:4 says, "Blessed are those who mourn, for they will be comforted." I gave comfort. I took her in as if she were my own. This little girl was the epitome of mourning. I had never seen such sadness and tragedy in just one little fragile vessel. Now she has taught me how much blessedness comes from comforting those who mourn. Blessedness—happiness, pleasure, contentment, or good fortune—does come to those who are mourning.

So how does one comfort those who mourn? I just held her in my arms and rocked her back and forth. I did not yet realize that the Sermon on the Mount is God's formula for revival. The Beatitudes are His recipe for His kingdom to come and His will to be done on the earth as it is in heaven.

Ministry is simply your loving as Jesus did. It is the Beatitudes manifested through your life. Missions are you ministering the love of God so that He can demonstrate His very life and nature through you. Missions are intended to be the Sermon on the Mount walked out on the earth.

If you find someone who is sick, help bring him healing. If you find someone who is hungry, feed him. If you find someone who is thirsty, give him water to drink. If you find someone naked, clothe him. If you find someone who is broken, weak, or weary, love him to wholeness. And if you find someone who is mourning, give him comfort.

Josina, another young girl who had a history of abuse and had nearly died from illness, made a difference in Camila's life. Because Josina understood suffering, she was also able to understand our beautiful, tiny, mute girl, Camila.

It was not complicated. I saw Josina stop for Camila. I remember watching the first time as Josina picked up Camila after she had been out of the hospital for only a few weeks. I watched day after day as she simply loved on that tiny girl.

She does not have a poster, a book, an itinerant circle, or a speaking schedule. But she has a ministry that brings the very heart of God to the heart of man on this earth. She traded her sorrow for His joy. She exchanged her ashes for His beauty. She learned to love.

Thought for Reflection

Loving as Jesus does isn't always an adventure. Sometimes it is just loving and feeding and clothing those God puts in front of you until they feel loved.

Prayer

Lord, whatever future You have for me, I need to love and comfort those around me. Teach me how to comfort the way Josina comforted Camila, the way You comfort those You love.

DAY 49
THE MIRACLE OF RESURRECTION

Therefore we were buried with Him by bap-
tism into death, that just as Christ was raised up
from the dead by the glory of the Father, even
so we also should walk in newness of life. For
if we have been united with Him in the like-
ness of His death, so shall we also be united
with Him in the likeness of His resurrection.
—ROMANS 5:4–5

When we talk about miracles in the charismatic Christian community, we often refer
to a person's recovering sight or hearing or
mobility. But sometimes miracles can be simply a little resurrection. Sometimes miracles
happen through baptism, through aligning
ourselves with Jesus's death and resurrection.

The day Josina and Camila were to be baptized, the queue was hundreds long. Suddenly I saw Camila. I looked down at her

and began questioning theologically, "Am I allowed to baptize this little girl? She doesn't talk. She doesn't speak."

I spoke to her, and I asked in her language, "Do you know what it means to die?" I said, "That's what baptism is. You have to die in this water and come up as a new creation. Your old life is going to die under water, and you will come up a new creation."

I saw her then, as usual, with tears streaming down her face. Using no words, she just nodded yes to me. She had no parents. She had no birth certificate. No one knew her age. And since being beaten and abused so many times, she still would not talk. I took this one little child into my arms, and in the name of the Father, His Son, Jesus, and the Holy Spirit, I put her tiny, frail body under that dirty green water. She came up beaming!

It was one of the greatest days of my life. Then Camila turned to me and spoke the very first words I ever heard her say: "Mama Aida, I want to lead the children's choir."

To me, that is ministry. I have watched countless times as the blind gain their sight. I am a witness nearly every week of my life as the deaf are able to hear. I have seen people whose limbs were once crippled walk again in complete wholeness. I see thousands run to my Jesus. But one of my greatest joys was to hear Camila speak for the first time! The simplicity of love healing a broken heart is what causes me to keep going.

Often we want the kingdom to look like multitudes who make our churches grow and make us look good. But the kingdom really looks like one smiling child at a time until nations are full of people who are passionate lovers of God. I look at Josina loving Camila back to life, and I think that is someone being raised from the dead! That's a resurrection.

Thought for Reflection

The love of Christ makes us new creations, heals our brokenness, and sets us free. If you set your mind on loving those you see with this kind of love, you will see miracles. Are you ready?

Prayer

Lord, You were able to heal Camila through the comfort she received and resurrect her through water baptism. Teach me how to love others with a love that can heal brokenness and bring about a miracle in their lives.

DAY 50
LET SUFFERING MAKE YOU LIKE JESUS

Blessed be God, the Father of our Lord Jesus Christ, the Father of mercies, and the God of all comfort, who comforts us in all our tribulation, that we may be able to comfort those who are in any trouble by the comfort with which we ourselves are comforted by God.
—2 CORINTHIANS 1:3–4

When you live in an affluent country, it is easy to think you are separate from suffering. After all, the masses are not hungry in America. However, we must acknowledge that all suffering is painful. The suffering in rich nations is loneliness. The suffering in rich nations is internal psychological pain. It is extremely relevant; it is deep. People feel it, and it is just as real as a bloated belly, people starving, or disease and death.

If we are to be Jesus's hands and feet, we

need to care about the needs of others—
internally and externally. The currency of
love in the West is not always money, but it
is always time and compassion. To heal an
orphaned or abandoned child in Mozambique takes a lot of love, a home, compassion,
and a bed and blankets. Of course, Coke and
chicken are a blessing for a feast! To heal an
orphaned or abandoned spirit in America
takes love, compassion, a lot of time, and undi-
vided attention toward one another. Both are
valid, both are real, and both are costly.

There is major suffering all over the world.
We can use our suffering to become more like
Jesus, or we can let bitterness fester inside our
hearts. Somehow, in God's mercy, He allows
us to understand the pain of others so that
we become more like Jesus in our compassion.
He can even use suffering because He knows
how to turn everything around for good.

Whatever you have experienced, you can
also sympathize with in others. If you have
been thirsty, you understand thirst. If you
have been lonely, you understand loneliness.
In the same way, we can also use our suffer-
ings to comfort those who are mourning. God

can use even the worst things from our lives and turn them into something good, if only we let Him. Josina is a perfect example. She uses the suffering of her past to love others.

Like Jesus's bride who is prepared in trials and tribulations, Josina stood proudly beaming in the center of our southern base on her wedding day. Her special celebration was a joyful occasion with all her friends. Now she calls the lost to the wedding feast of the ages. She is filling the Father's house by sharing Jesus with all her friends. This is the gospel. This is a girl who knows the blessings of both mourning and comforting. She knows how to be love incarnate to those around her.

Thought for Reflection

A minister is simply a sent one. You might be sent only across the street, but it does not matter. Bring love and comfort to those around you, wherever you are. To God, whether it is to one or the masses, it is the same—it is His love incarnate. What painful experience have you had that will help you to comfort others in similar situations?

Prayer

Lord, I want to acknowledge the suffering of all. Let me bring comfort to those who need it and be a light in their lives. Teach me the blessing of using my own suffering to help me understand and comfort others.

DAY 51
SEE THROUGH THE
EYES OF JESUS

Then Peter came to Him and said, "Lord, how often shall I forgive my brother who sins against me? Up to seven times?" Jesus said to him, "I do not say to you up to seven times, but up to seventy times seven."
—MATTHEW 18:21–22

Have you ever met individuals so difficult it feels impossible to love them? People who push you away and hurt you? Was it hard to forgive them and to keep loving them? I've been in this situation; it is never fun. But then I get to see God change hearts.

I met a girl while preaching on the streets of London. I will call her Jennifer. She was so angry that she basically hated everyone, especially men. She had been gang-raped by sixteen men. She had to stay in the hospital for nearly a year with complications from a broken pelvis, and she had no family or friends.

She was tormented by hatred and demons, but I loved Jennifer.

I also made another friend—I will call him Daniel. Almost every single day for several years I would go talk to Daniel and bring him food. He would yell and tell me to go away and curse at me. He did this for two and a half years. With each curse, I thought how much this man needed love, kindness, and mercy.

I refused to stop. Jesus is tenacious: He never stops loving, and He never stops giving. I just kept saying, "I love you, Daniel, and Jesus loves you." God's heart is relentless, and His radical love transforms the hardest of hearts.

One night Jennifer was so angry, she tried to beat me to death. Even in this hateful act, I felt God's heart for her. I tried to tell her, "God is in love with you. You are precious. You are called to know His love." My words made her angrier!

Then Daniel, who had been watching me get beaten the whole time, said he was calling the police. I told him the Lord did not want me to call them. Daniel just screamed and cursed at me again.

I felt so tired; I could not take any more

pain. I told Jennifer, "If you are going to kill me, you can just kill me. But I have to sit down."

Just as I prayed, Daniel came and rescued me. He grabbed me away from Jennifer and started sobbing, and then he said, "For two years you told me Jesus loved me. Now I've seen His love, and I want Him. I want Him now. You kept telling me about love, but today I have seen love."

That night Daniel fell to his knees and received Jesus as his Lord. The following week Jennifer came to my house with a dozen roses for me, and she told me that she was sorry for trying to kill me. That day she asked Jesus to live in her heart too.

Many people recognize only each other's faults rather than choosing to see the image of God. Hope colors the way we see each other. Grace is the lens through which we must see one another. When we look at someone, we have to look beyond the evil of the past. We have to look through the blood of Jesus into the heart of every man—we have to peer through the eyes of the Master.

He commands us to forgive seventy times seven, telling us that love "always protects, always trusts, always hopes, always perseveres" (1 Cor. 13:7, NIV). His blood is more than enough.

Thought for Reflection

Consider how you respond to difficult people. Do you ignore them? Are you rude in return? Or do you see them through Jesus's eyes as ones who need His love?

Prayer

Lord, teach me to see difficult people through the eyes of grace and to respond to them in love. Help me not to give up on them, even when they don't at first receive my efforts to demonstrate Your love.

WALK IN THE ANOINTING GOD GAVE YOU

*For we are His workmanship, created in Christ
Jesus for good works, which God prepared
beforehand, so that we should walk in them.*
—EPHESIANS 2:10

As a parent, have you ever tried to model one child after another? Have you attempted to make one child more like his sibling or a friend's youngster? If you have, you know your efforts were futile. Every child is unique in his personality, just as each child of God is unique in his gifts and calling.

Each one of us has a particular calling from the Lord. Once we have imbibed the lavishness of His love, we will find the greatest possible satisfaction in walking the unique path He sets. Do not try to copy someone else's calling. It is very difficult to dance ballet while wearing boots. If He gave you ballet shoes, dance ballet; if He gave you lumberjack boots, cut down trees.

I know what it is like to try on the sort of anointing that belongs to someone else. I tried once, at a large conference. I had decided I should make my next message a properly sophisticated one. I spent hours crafting a sermon, but when I got in front of the audience, the Holy Spirit overwhelmed me. "I do not have sophistication. I do not have some snazzy words or notes and quotes. I am just a laid-down lover. All I want to do is love Him," I told them.

I tried one more time to prepare myself for speaking with notes and quotes. I headed to a bookstore to get some references but fell down under the weighty glory of God right between the shelves. On the bookstore floor I had another vision. I felt God telling me to look at my feet, so I glanced down. I was wearing huge clown shoes. They were so ridiculous and so comically oversized that I could not have walked anywhere in them. Then I sensed the Lord speak very clearly that I ought not to wear anyone else's shoes. He desires that each one of His sons and daughters walk in the tailor-made shoes He has for them. There is a specific destiny and anointing for each one. It is as useless to try to be someone else as it is for me to try to walk comfortably in big clown shoes.

Many ministers are brilliant with their words. They can do amazing things with sermon structure, research, and oratory. They can do all the notes and quotes. That is a wonderful gift—but I cannot preach the way they do because God gave me different gifts. He has prepared good works for each of us; do those good works and don't worry about doing someone else's (Eph. 2:10).

He is the One who makes us free to be ourselves, and that freedom has a purpose. Each of us has an authority that is unique to us and also a specific field to harvest. To reap the harvest, we need to use the authority He gives us.

The shoes He made for you will not fit anyone else. Fill them.

Thought for Reflection

We need to understand who we are. If we want to bear fruit for God, we must be willing to risk being the people He truly made us to be—even when we do not perform the way others expect. Whose shoes do you need to remove today in order to put on your own?

Prayer

Lord, I want to be the person You created me to be. Help me to accept myself and step out to fill the specific calling You have placed on my life.

DAY 53
WHATEVER YOU DO, GLORIFY GOD

Therefore, whether you eat, or drink, or what-
ever you do, do it all to the glory of God.
—1 CORINTHIANS 10:31

God designed each of us to have a unique calling. He may have appointed you to be a missionary, a teacher, an evangelist, or an intercessor who spends hours each day in prayer. Whatever the calling is, your fulfilling it pleases God.

When I preach, bring home a dying child, or show love to someone who is broken inside, I feel God's pleasure. That is what I am created to do. I used to not want to go anywhere outside Mozambique. My favorite place was the garbage dump, and that was that. It did not matter if I was staying in a five-star hotel—being anywhere outside my corner of Africa made me agitated and discontent.

The dirt does not bother me. But because God is making me more and more free every day, I have also learned to be happy wherever I go. I know I can glorify Him wherever I am, regardless what I am doing. As long as God sends me, I choose to rejoice. On His errands I get to dream what He dreams. I get to be whatever He calls me to be.

I encourage you to reflect on the calling God has given you. Do not worry about what calling He has given someone else. What is it that you want to do? Who do you want to become? For what do you want to be known? If you have never asked the Holy Spirit to speak to you about these things, I encourage you to spend time doing so now. You will never be happier than when you know the unique destiny His love has prepared for your life.

Whether you believe it or not, the truth is that you are a child of God. Whether you are an engineer, scientist, medical doctor, psychiatrist, nurse, preacher, architect, or housewife, He has lovingly created you to fulfill a unique purpose that will glorify Him. Therefore "whatever you do, do it all for the glory of God" (1 Cor. 10:31). Whether you are called to the poor or to the wealthy, to lonely children on your local street or to the students of Ivy League universities, your destiny is to reflect the Father's light to this world in a way only you can.

If you get it all wrong, He will pick you up, swing you around in His arms, and correct you. He will hug you and put you back on your feet. That is how God behaves toward His children. He will dance with you. He will smile as He gazes on your beautiful face. He will lavish His love on you until it overflows.

Thought for Reflection

Do you know what it is God is calling you to do? Do you wonder if your calling is less important than another's? Have hope: God is glorified in whatever way you serve Him. Seek to do so joyfully.

Prayer

Lord, I accept Your calling on my life. I understand that by fulfilling it, I am pleasing You. Please use what I do to bring You glory.

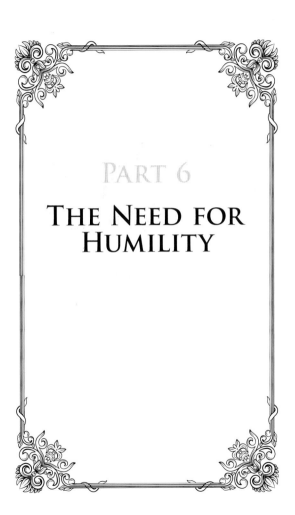

PART 6

THE NEED FOR HUMILITY

DAY 54
JESUS MODELED HUMILITY

Let this mind be in you all, which was also in Christ Jesus, who, being in the form of God, did not consider equality with God something to be grasped. But He emptied Himself, taking upon Himself the form of a servant, and was made in the likeness of men. And being found in the form of a man, He humbled Himself and became obedient to death, even death on a cross.
—PHILIPPIANS 2:5–8

Have you ever been humbled? Most of us have been, and it usually is not an experience we are eager to repeat. Being humbled by others can bring shame and humiliation.

Humbling ourselves can be painful too—in a different way. It requires giving up our own comfort and desires in order to fulfill God's will for us. However, it is essential preparation for serving others.

When we go on outreaches in rural Africa,

our village hosts frequently stun us with hospitality. They give us their very best. This generally means staying in a one-room mud hut with their children—along with a few chickens and maybe a rooster.

The roosters never seem to know what time it is. I have lost count of the number of times I have laid my head down, ready to fall asleep after a long night of preaching, only to hear a confused rooster, in the pitch dark, suddenly crow right in my ear: "Cock-a-doodle-doo!" Talk about humbling.

This is the kind of humility Jesus modeled for us.

The King of glory gave up all He was in heaven to pour out all He is here on earth. God emptied Himself, left heaven, and made Himself vulnerable. The Bible says that "for the joy that was set before Him" (Heb. 12:2), the Lamb of God endured the price of His mission, which culminated in the scorn of the cross. He left behind streets of gold and all the splendor of heaven.

I believe He gave up knowledge, as well. Do you suppose Jesus came out of the womb knowing everything and said, "Follow Me; I am the Son of God"? I don't think so. The Creator of the universe chose to become completely empty. When He came out of the womb, He needed to be nursed at His mother's breast. He was dependent on her for everything, even His very life. The Son of God had to learn how to walk and how to talk. He had to learn a language. He needed those around Him to teach Him the most basic tools of life in Judea. He became a student. When He did this, He was modeling for us the beauty of dependence.

Our King was born to a young woman in a dirty stable full of domestic animals. It might seem an improper or disgraceful way for a king to be born, but for love's sake God humbled Himself.

I did not grow up in this kind of environment, but I have come to understand a little about life in the dirt. I understand some of the circumstances into which Jesus was born. When I am drifting off to sleep in a mud hut with two or three children on a rough rope bed next to me, trying to ignore the rooster brushing against my head, I feel the joy of the Lord. Oftentimes there is not enough grass on the roof. When I look up, I can see the clear African sky, free of city lights, full of stars. I call this my billion-star hotel.

Thought for Reflection

Are you open to living a life of humility, willing to go wherever God calls you and to do whatever He asks? Will you empty yourself out as Jesus emptied Himself out? What is keeping you from taking this step?

Prayer

Lord, I know it will be difficult to live a life of humility as You did. But I want to be like You so that You can use me to minister to others. Help me to be willing to give up whatever is necessary.

DAY 55
DEPENDENCE ON GOD

My soul, wait silently for God, for my hope is from Him. He only is my rock and my salvation; He is my refuge; I will not be moved. In God is my salvation and my glory; the rock of my strength, and my shelter, is in God. Trust in Him at all times; you people, pour out your heart before Him; God is a shelter for us.
—PSALM 62:5–8

As we grow up, we all like to become independent. We want to live on our own and take care of ourselves. Spiritually, however, dependence is necessary. Relying on God is necessary. Nothing I do, none of my work in Mozambique, is because of me; it is all because of God.

When I spent a week on the floor in Canada without being able to walk or talk, God taught me a profound lesson in dependence. I didn't like being unable to get up and move around as I pleased; I didn't like being unable to speak or even to go the restroom by myself. My extreme need for other people was uncomfortable and inconvenient. I felt very vulnerable. For seven days I literally could not do anything without some fellow member of the body of Christ being there to pick me up and take me where I needed to be.

During this time I felt the Lord telling me I was always moving, but now was the time to stop, be still, and rest. He just wanted me to lie on the floor and let Him love me. He held me in His weighty glory. He slowed me down so I couldn't move outside His presence. He spoke beautiful words to me and made me still.

It remained uncomfortable to be stuck on the floor with no control over myself, but I replied to Him, "Yes, Lord, I yield to Your will!" Of course, I still wanted to move, but I didn't fight Him. Sometimes I found myself thinking I really wanted a drink, and someone I didn't know would come and bring me a glass of water.

God had captured all my attention. He told me I could do nothing without Him and nothing without His body. He was germinating something powerful, causing my own little heart and vision to expand to a bursting point. I believe He was causing my inability to become His ability. I believe God, by His Holy Spirit, overshadowed me and planted a nation inside me.

How does He do that?

Who can say?

He is God, and He does whatever He likes. He will use anyone, even a little mama like me. God can use anybody who is yielded, who is in love with Him, and who says yes.

Thought for Reflection

Are you comfortable admitting your utter dependence on God? Do you acknowledge that you can do nothing worthwhile without Him? Give in to Him today, and allow Him to overshadow you so you can rest in His presence and acknowledge your need for Him.

Prayer

Lord, I need You. I acknowledge that without You and Your provision I can do nothing. Show me how to live in utter dependence on You.

Day 56
Blessed Are the Poor in Spirit

Blessed are the poor in spirit, for
theirs is the kingdom of heaven.
—MATTHEW 5:3

We can learn a lot from the poor. They draw us into a life of living even lower still, leading us on the low road until we become as desperate for God as they are for daily bread. When we send our international visitors home from Mozambique, we always pray that they take home the riches of the poor because, as Matthew 5:3 says, "Blessed are the poor in spirit, for theirs is the kingdom of heaven."

What does it mean to be poor in spirit? There is something about the poor that delights the heart of God. They are contrite. They know they are in need. But what is it about them that draws the kingdom of God to the earth? The answer to this question

216

lies in their dependency, hunger, need, and desperation.

When I was in my twenties, God stopped me and told me to sit with the poor. He hid me for years in the slums, tucked away to deal with my self-sufficiency and undo any backup plan or I-can-do-it-myself attitude. He brought me to the poor to learn. The poor made me rich; in so many ways they were my mentors in the things of the Spirit. For years while we lived there in Asia, Jesus came to me every day in the faces of those poor.

Jesus is always enough. He died so we could all be adopted by His Father. I always pray a great phrase in Swahili, *Shika Baba*, which means "hold on to the Father." We can trust our Father's love for us in the middle of pain and suffering.

I heard God call me to bring the lost home to my Father's house. In those slums I learned to do this very thing and be totally dependent on Him. I learned how to hold on to the heart of the King no matter how difficult a situation was. I learned that my Father really looks after me.

I believe that when Jesus used the phrase

"poor in spirit," He was referring to a posturing of the heart in which one is wholly given, fully yielded, completely desperate, and totally dependent on God alone. It doesn't require you to be penniless. The Lord wants to cause even the rich and the middle class to be poor in spirit and to know that they are in total need of Him.

God visits those who want Him. The wealthiest people and cultures often experience fewer miracles and less of the supernatural not because they are rich but because they are self-reliant and therefore not aware of their need for Him.

Thought for Reflection

Being poor in spirit is not about being poor in the world's eyes. It is about living low, living humbled, and being desperate for God. It is about understanding your absolute need for Him. Do you know how much you need Him? Do you live as if you are totally dependent on Him?

Prayer

Lord, help me to learn from those You send me to. Show me how to live completely dependent on You, waiting for You and trusting You to show up. You are always enough for any situation.

DAY 57
NO BACKUP PLAN

Then you shall call upon Me, and you shall
come and pray to Me, and I will listen to
you. You shall seek Me and find Me, when
you shall search for Me with all your heart.
—JEREMIAH 29:12–13

It is important to recognize how utterly dependent on God you are. You must lean on Him completely in every area of your life—doing nothing out of self and having no backup plan.

Since moving to Mozambique, we have learned to depend on God for everything. If He does not show up, we are dead. What we need most is to be totally dependent on God's showing up. We need His pure presence.

In our poor Mozambican mud-hut churches we have to have God show up—and we have to have fresh food—or no one will come. People wouldn't want to come to church for the carpets because, even if we had them, they would be full of dirt and bugs! People come to church to dance, to rejoice, to sing, to meet with God, and to be healed and delivered.

If God doesn't show up, no one else will either. If God does not heal, we will be dead. If God does not deliver, demons will torment the people to death. We have no fund-raising backup scheme. If God does not take care of our children and provide for our needs, we can't and won't go on.

Each day we depend on Him for our daily bread to feed the multitudes. We rely on God. In Jesus we have all that we need. He died that there would be more than enough. We watch God multiply food to feed the masses, just as Jesus took a few fish and loaves of bread to feed the hungry. We watch God touch hearts to give to the needy. We try to stop for every single sick, hurting, or dying person we find in front of us. For months during the floods in Mozambique we fed tens of thousands of people a day. And we see food multiply as the churches are filled with hungry and desperate people.

I finally am beginning to understand God's kingdom from the children and the poor. They teach us about dependence, humility, and being emptied of all else so that God can fill us. They simply have nothing else.

We know that we have no ability within ourselves. We have no PowerPoint presentations to display. We are grateful if we sometimes have electricity! There are no glossy brochures or slick side items. What we do have are national and foreign workers giving their lives as God's instruments. And we appreciate every gift and talent they bring.

God hears the cry of the poor even when we are not all pure in heart. He opens our ears to hear the cries of the hungry children, and He softens our hearts toward them—to help them. He honors our faith in Him and our desperation to do whatever is necessary. God's compassion meets us in our desperation.

Thought for Reflection

In some ways, the poor are blessed because they are acutely aware of their need. We all live in that need. We all need His presence. We all need Him to move in our lives and ministries. Are you willing to give up your backup plan and rely completely on Him?

Prayer

Lord, make me aware of how much I truly need You. Thank You for always being there and for always being enough.

DAY 58
WE NEED ONE ANOTHER

For you know the grace of our Lord Jesus
Christ, that though He was rich, yet for
your sakes He became poor, that through
His poverty you might be rich.
—2 CORINTHIANS 8:9

As I have, you have undoubtedly entered into a situation with the goal of helping others, excited about how God is going to use you, only to realize afterward that you learned more and received more than you gave. God often uses those to whom we minister to teach us as well. We give, but we also receive; and in the economy of God, we need both to survive.

Why does the kingdom break forth in such power among the poor here in Mozambique? It's because the poor rely on one another. They need one another. They live in a community of interdependence. They have to share with one another just to survive. Those who have much are often quick to accumulate and slow to give away. Yet those who have little are quick to share. They often give without remembering; they receive without forgetting. The poor are truly rich for the simplicity of their devotion.

I did not move to Mozambique with an action plan to save the country. My goal was not to start a revival. My vision was not to oversee thousands of churches. I came to learn to love, and I am still just at the beginning of that journey today. I am just starting to learn how to love more. I believe this is my lifetime goal. I want to love God with everything within me. I want to love my neighbor as myself.

When God sent me to the poor, it was not for what I could give, but for what I could learn and for what I could receive. God did not start by telling me to minister *to* the poor but to be ministered to *by* them. Mother Teresa said:

> Today it is very fashionable to talk about the poor. Unfortunately, it is not fashionable to talk with them.[1]

We need to start talking with them. The poor are my friends and my family. Village life is quite simple compared to Western culture. I love to camp in the mud-hut villages and enjoy the simplicity of the poor. We sing and dance into the night, worshipping our beautiful Jesus. There are no computers, videos, CD players, or electricity to distract us. It is simple but heartfelt devotion.

The poor have taught me that we must receive just to live.

Thought for Reflection

In every situation, even when (or maybe especially when) serving the lowest of the low, the poorest of the poor, be looking for what the Lord is teaching you. Learn from those you serve about God's love and grace.

Prayer

Lord, use the situations I am in to teach me about You and about how to serve You. Even when I am serving others, let me always be learning how to love better.

Day 59
CHILDLIKE FAITH

Jesus called a little child to Him and set him in their midst, and said, "Truly I say to you, unless you are converted and become like little children, you will not enter the kingdom of heaven. Therefore whoever humbles himself like this little child is the greatest in the kingdom of heaven."
—MATTHEW 18:2–4

Little children truly have keys to the kingdom. They are more trusting than adults. Children believe in miracles until they are taught by some adult that believing in things unseen is silliness. A four-year-old child in any culture has faith in miracles. Then an adult comes along and teaches him not to believe.

I have learned so much from my mentors— the poor and the children. As Mother Teresa said, "He wants us to be more childlike, more humble, more grateful in prayer, to remember we all belong to the mystical body of Christ."[1]

I feel the love and comfort of God through my children. Our children are our ministry team for our village outreaches. Through their childlike faith, miracles are on the increase. Recently in a village in the "bush" of Cabo Delgado, hundreds of people were giving their lives to Jesus. Then one of our missionaries brought a deaf boy to the children. After we all prayed, he was instantly healed. Yes, the kingdom of God belongs to the children!

I have a hunger for Jesus that is satisfied only as we find more children to take in, as they teach us about the nature of our Father.

At our Pemba base with these new children whom we love, we often have baby dedications and weddings. On the weekends, after dinner, we take ten of our own children to our house for a sleepover. We are watching Jesus transform their little orphaned and abandoned spirits into full spirits of sonship. We are seeing God raise up an army of preachers and pastors out of the streets and the garbage dumps.

These children are our inheritance on

earth. We love them dearly. Surely the king-dom belongs to such as these!

Thought for Reflection

Jesus said we would not enter the king-dom of heaven unless we become like little children. We need their faith, their humility, their unwavering trust in God. Are these qualities you can lay claim to today, or do you need the Holy Spirit to work them in you?

Prayer

Lord, help me to become more childlike in my faith. Help me to trust You and to step out without fear to accomplish Your work as they do. Thank You for their example.

Day 60
Trusting God to Fulfill His Word

*For all the promises of God in Him are "Yes," and
in Him "Amen," to the glory of God through us.*
—2 Corinthians 1:20

Perhaps you are as perplexed as I have been at
some of God's promises, wondering how they
could possibly come to pass. I was particularly
skeptical when God promised me "hundreds
of churches" in Mozambique. But remember what happened when the angel of the
Lord made the most outrageous and incredible promise to Mary. Despite the impossible
nature of that word, Mary chose to believe it.
"I am the servant of the Lord," she said. "May
it be unto me according to your word" (Luke
1:38). You too can believe God and receive the
promises He makes to you.

Just after I returned home from the conference where I was stood on my head, where

God promised He was turning my ministry upside down, there was massive flooding in Mozambique. In some places there were almost forty days and nights of rain. Water rushed through and covered a huge swath of the country, including hundreds of towns and villages. Thousands of people died—first from the flooding, then from cholera and other water-borne illnesses, and finally from exposure and starvation.

We had a lot of sleepless nights that month. One of our centers was completely covered in water. The staff had to carry the boys and girls to safety on their shoulders. During the evacuation ten of them were stranded and had to sit out the worst of the flooding in the tops of trees.

Wherever we had resources, we tried to reach as many flood victims as we could. We drove out into the mud and water until our trucks were being washed away along with the roads. After that we walked. Refugee camps were springing up everywhere. People beyond count had lost their homes. Some foreign aid organizations came, but there were more hungry people than they could deal with.

We began to feed as many as we could. We did our best to feed them natural and spiritual bread and found out the nation was extremely hungry for God. People started coming to Jesus by the hundreds and thousands.

Soon United Nations representatives came and asked us how many of their helicopters we wanted to use. They would lend us five to seven helicopters a day! We sent them out with food and preachers. Thousands of churches were birthed while the floodwaters still stood.

In some places food was supernaturally multiplied. Once, a bulk shipping vessel entirely filled with containers of food came without warning and unloaded supplies for us. There was no central plan. It was a terrible time, but the positive fruit far exceeded anything we knew to expect. Who would have guessed that God would use such a tragic situation to fulfill His promise to me and plant churches throughout the country?

Thought for Reflection

Do you trust God when He gives you promises, even when they seem outlandish and impossible? Do you doubt that He is able or that He wants to fulfill them? Dare to believe and receive, and watch how He comes through.

Prayer

Lord, I commit to praying over the promises You have given me. Though they seem far-fetched to my human mind, amaze me in the ways You fulfill them.

DAY 61
MARY'S EXAMPLE

He has shown strength with His arm; He has scattered the proud in the imagination of their hearts. He has pulled down the mighty from their thrones and exalted those of low degree. He has filled the hungry with good things, and the rich He has sent away empty. He has helped His servant Israel, in remembrance of His mercy, as He spoke to our fathers, to Abraham and to his descendants forever.
—LUKE 1:51–55

As we journey through this life, the Lord will put us in situations we don't fully understand. He will ask us to give birth to promises that seem impossible. It takes humility to nurture something that is beyond your understanding while counting it all as joy. Mary's response to God's word—the song she sang after she learned what she'd been asked to do—can light our way. It held joy and humility close together. She was undone.

She had not sought greatness. Her celebration grew from brokenness. Part of her may have wanted to run from this promise that was too great for comprehension, but instead she said yes.

Her reward was the Son of God.

Mary rejoiced in the Lord, but I think she was also required to give grace and mercy to those who judged her when her condition became clear. Sometimes enduring persecution is the way we glorify God in the midst of the incomprehensible and the miraculous.

We may not have enough strength in us to do this, but Mary shows us how to do it supernaturally. We focus on the One who is altogether lovely. We gaze upon the beauty of the Lord and worship Him alone. Then He will cause supernatural strength to come upon us. He will give us grace to pay the cost with joy. He will empower us to bless those who slander us. Because of Him we are able to show mercy to our enemies.

We cannot cause anything to be birthed in ourselves. Without Him our efforts produce nothing spectacular, no matter how much we strive. The one thing we can do is respond to the Father's words over our lives. We can position our hearts in humility and hunger. Hunger always delights the heart of God.

People often ask me why we see so many more miracles among the poor than among wealthy, comfortable westerners. The answer is simple: The poor know they are in need. They know what it is to be desperate and hungry, and they turn that desperation and hunger toward Him. They stay desperate. They stay hungry. God lifts up the humble, and He fills the hungry with good things (Luke 1:52–53).

Thought for Reflection

When you are in a difficult situation, stay humble; stay hungry. It is your humility before God and your hunger for Him that allow Him to move in miraculous ways. Stay humble and hungry even through difficulties and misunderstandings, and watch God move in your life.

Prayer

Lord, when I don't understand my circumstances, I know You are still with me. Help me to trust, stay humble, and stay hungry for You—especially when life isn't going as I had planned.

Day 62
Blessed Are the Meek

Blessed are the meek, for they shall inherit the earth.
—MATTHEW 5:5

The point is not you—the point is Him. The point is not me—the point is Him. He alone is worthy of glory. Sometimes He offends our minds to reveal our hearts and make us into fools. I feel like God's little fool; He reduced me to the simplicity of love.

God once told me, "If I can get pastors and ministers to lay down, I can turn the world upside down." God was talking about laying down or giving up the desire for the "things" of this world. He is looking for servants who are so hungry that they desire Him more than their very lives. They have not arrived. There is no arriving. They consider it all a loss for the surpassing greatness of knowing Christ Jesus (Phil. 3:7). God is less concerned with our being powerful and more concerned with our being willing.

Before I preach somewhere, a staff member often prays a prayer over me that asks, "Lord, make Heidi into a little paintbrush in Your hands, and paint whatever You want in her life laid down." We must all be pliable in the Master's hands. He wants to turn us upside down in order to turn the world upside down (Acts 17:6).

God is saying, "Lay down more. Lay down." So there is only one direction in ministry: lower still.

One man, who has a high position on our staff, is the perfect example of going lower. There is much more to this man than just his position. Papa Surpresa moves in many miracles but never seems to be prideful. He is a meek, humble man who laughs easily and is filled with joy. Though he is anointed with great authority and has seen the dead raised, it is joy, humility, and meekness that crown him.

One of the first things you notice when you meet Surpresa is his teeth because he is always smiling. He is joyful all the time, even in difficult circumstances. We were recently on a healing outreach in the bush where we had a visitor who was used to sleeping in nice hotels. Looking up at the African sky, Surpresa simply smiled at the well-known itinerant who was about to sleep outside and said, "You are used to being in the Holiday Inn. We are in the Holiday Out. You know the five-star hotels? We are in the million-star hotel!"

When you are humble, you can live in a five-star hotel or under a million stars in the bush and count it all as joy. Matthew 5:5 says, "Blessed are the meek, for they will inherit the earth." One meaning of that scripture is that you are always rich because you are abiding in the very heart of God. There is something about the humble that allows Jesus to flow out of their lives. We see the fingerprint of God in their humble frames.

Psalm 2:8 says, "Ask of Me, and I will make the nations your inheritance, and the ends of the earth your possession." What type of earth do the meek inherit? Is this passage describing material prosperity? I believe it is describing the new earth. But God will also entrust the meek with inheriting different people groups as His possession. It is friends, children, and family who are our true riches. And He has given me my Mozambican family as my inheritance.

Thought for Reflection

God is calling us to lay down our desire for the things of this world. He is calling us to serve from a place of humility and meekness. When we do this, we will inherit the earth. What inheritance are you looking for?

Prayer

Lord, as You move me forward in the promises You have placed on my life, remind me that this is all about You. This is not about me, my authority, or my position; it is all about bringing You glory.

DAY 63
THE KEY TO TRULY
BEING FULL

Humble yourselves in the sight of the
Lord, and He will lift you up.
—JAMES 4:10

Think about the spiritual leaders you know. Are they in ministry for themselves, trying to make it on their own and looking for recognition and rewards on this earth? Or are they humbling themselves as Jesus did and working only for the glory of God?

Selfish ambition is the mortal enemy of the heart of the church. That is why the very first beatitude is an exhortation to be poor in spirit, in complete awareness of our desperate need for Jesus. Without this revelation, little blessing will flow.

When I was in my twenties, I still had some ambition and self-reliance. I thought it was really exciting to be invited to do big meetings. I remember when Jesus stopped me. I was preaching all over Asia, seeing hundreds, sometimes thousands, of people come to Jesus night after night.

Then God said, "Stop!" But I rebuked that voice in Jesus's name, thinking it was the enemy. The third time I heard the voice, I realized it was God, and I fell on my face. I had to ask God why He would tell me to stop when I was leading "the multitudes" to Him. He told me, "You don't know anything about the kingdom." I did not want to hear that.

So I told God that I did know about His kingdom. After all, people were coming to Jesus. He again said to me, "You don't know about the kingdom." Finally I decided to start listening. That's when He told me to sit with the poor and learn.

God cannot use selfish ambition. He cannot bless vain conceit. He wants to rip it out of us.

In humility you consider others to be better than yourself. You never put yourself in the high place above others; for example, one of the first things I often do in big conferences or outdoor meetings, if possible, is take down the red ropes barricading me from the people.

I look at all the bodyguards and laugh, saying, "No ropes!" I do appreciate their help, however, when I am really tired. But most of the time, I sit in the dirt or on the floor with everyone else.

Our pastors here in Mozambique do not have lovely clothes or fine leather shoes. They live in mud huts. We call them "papas" rather than "apostles" or "reverends." But they are like the early apostles "…who have turned the world upside down" (Acts 17:6).

One of my favorite heroes in the faith has raised three people from the dead and oversees a region in our movement with her husband. Everywhere they preach, great signs and wonders follow. She couldn't read or write very well, so she was not able to pass her Bible school exams. Of course we graduated her anyway because anyone with that level of faith, love and compassion is surely ready to be a pastor!

Think about that: three people were raised from the dead, but she can barely read or write. Perhaps God does not care as much about our qualifications as we do! She is just one of the meek ones who have inherited the earth in God's upside-down economy.

Thought for Reflection

It is easy to be tempted in ministry to think you can work on your own power, that you are bearing fruit because of yourself. Have you fought this temptation? Guard against it in your life and ministry; know that all you have and all the good you do comes from Him.

Prayer

Lord, teach me first how little I truly know about You and Your kingdom and rid me of selfish ambition; then teach me what I need to know about You to move into what You have for me.

DAY 64
FEAR THE LORD

My soul magnifies the Lord, and my spirit
rejoices in God my Savior. For He has regarded
the low estate of His servant; surely, from now
on all generations will call me blessed. For He
who is mighty has done great things for me, and
holy is His name. His mercy is on those who
fear Him from generation to generation.

—LUKE 1:46–50

Many Christians don't understand what it means to "fear the Lord." They think we are to shrink from Him because of His wrath. But just as we need hunger and humility, we need a holy fear to carry God's promises to full term. Mary sang, "His mercy is on those who fear Him from generation to genera-tion" (Luke 1:50). I believe the essence of this necessary fear is that we must never seek to take His glory for ourselves. May we always carry His presence and bear within us the very promises of the Most High God—but may we never, ever touch His glory!

Psalm 33:8 says "let all the earth fear the LORD" and declares that everyone—"all the inhabitants of the world"—should "stand in awe of Him." You must stand in awe of Him and fear Him rather than acting and living as if you are responsible for the good things in your life and in your ministry.

"His mercy extends to those who fear Him"—that is the response we are to have when God comes upon us and gives us prophetic promises. No matter how much we have fasted, sacrificed, or toiled, we cannot boast in what we do. We produce nothing alone. I know that I can do nothing without the Lord and nothing without His body, but if I will lie down and love the One who is worthy—if I will fear Him, trust Him, and have faith in Him—His mercy upon a jar of clay like me will be enough to let me carry some of His glory to a lost and dying world.

Thought for Reflection

When you hear the phrase "fear the Lord," what comes to mind? Have you explored this idea in the past? Think about it again. Do you fear the Lord? Do you have a healthy respect for and awe of His power, His authority? Fear Him, knowing you can do nothing under your own power, nothing apart from Him, and He will show you mercy.

Prayer

Lord, I live in awe and holy fear of You. Let everything I do bring You alone glory and honor.

PART 7

DON'T GIVE UP

DAY 65
NURTURE THE PROMISES OF GOD

Rejoice always. Pray without ceasing. In every-thing give thanks, for this is the will of God in Christ Jesus concerning you. Do not quench the Spirit. Do not despise prophecies. Exam-ine all things. Firmly hold onto what is good. Abstain from all appearances of evil.
—1 THESSALONIANS 5:16–22

Do you know people who always expect great things to happen but never take any steps to make them happen? Say you want to be a third-grade teacher. If you don't go to college, apply yourself in class, learn how to work with children, and pass your state licen-sure exam, you will never become a third-grade teacher.

When the Lord told me I would be a min-ister, I did not wake up overseas one day in a brand-new church. I had to buy my ticket, get on a plane, and go preach in the slums. When the Lord told me I would get a graduate degree, no one mailed it to me. I had to apply, study for four years, write a thesis, and take many difficult exams.

Walking out the promises of God means making practical decisions. Mary received a supernatural promise, but she still had to care for her baby. The baby growing inside her needed her loving care in order to thrive. To begin with, she needed to rest, eat well, and take care of herself.

If a mother wants a healthy baby, she eats what is good for her and for her child. Likewise, we have to be careful not to kill or damage our "babies"—our promises— with bad "food" such as negative attitudes, criticism, backbiting, unbelief, or agitation. These things will not do our "babies" good. As Philippians 4:8 says, "Whatever things are true, whatever things are honest, whatever things are just, whatever things are pure, whatever things are lovely, whatever things are of good report, if there is any virtue, and if there is any praise, think on these things." This is the right kind of food. We need to nurture that which God puts inside us with the right kind of food.

Most of all we all need to spend time in the secret place. We are nourished by prayer, by Scripture, and by the body of Christ.

There may also be more specific food your baby needs. For example, if God has called you to be a healing evangelist, you may need to read about great healing evangelists of the past. You may need to find a mentor with a particular gift for healing. You may need to move to a place where you can learn more and practice. Whatever it takes, eat the food that will make your baby grow.

Thought for Reflection

Think about the promises God has given you. Are there practical steps you must take for these promises to be fulfilled? Even if their "birth dates" seem far off, what small steps can you take to bring them a little closer?

Prayer

Lord, I release any negative things in my spirit right now: bad attitudes, unbelief, bitterness. Remove them from my heart and fill me with thanksgiving for the promises You have given me. Help me to do whatever You direct to nurture them to fulfillment.

DAY 66
PRESS INTO THE PROMISE

*Let us firmly hold the profession of our faith
without wavering, for He who promised is
faithful. And let us consider how to spur
one another to love and to good works.*
—HEBREWS 10:23–24

Have you ever struggled to believe in something God has promised? It can be difficult to remain steadfast and to hold on to the promises of God when it seems as if nothing is happening.

For many years I longed to witness healing miracles—for the blind to see, the deaf to hear, the dumb to speak, and the cripples to walk. I was living in the slums and working with the poorest people I could find, so I saw these kinds of afflictions often. My heart was continually broken for them.

Eventually I received a promise from the Lord that the blind *would* see and my nation *would* be transformed. For a year after this I prayed for every single blind person I found.

Not one of them saw.

But I did not give up. I knew I had been overshadowed for this purpose. I had faith. As Hebrews says, "He who promised is faithful" (Heb. 10:23). I kept looking for more and more blind people. I would ask for them to come forward at every meeting. If I saw one by the road, I would leap out of my truck and lay my hands on them. Almost everyone I prayed for got saved, but for the longest time no one gained vision.

And then one day God's promise began to be manifest.

I was in a dark little mud-hut church in central Mozambique, laying my hands on an old blind lady. Her eyes were clouded, the irises and pupils totally white. Suddenly, as I was praying for her, she fell down on the dirt floor. I watched her eyes go from white to gray and then to dark, shiny brown. After all the years of hoping, crying, and trying, I witnessed what I had waited for. The woman could see!

Delighted beyond words, I asked her, "What's your name?"

She said, "Mama Aida."

"My name is Mama Aida too!" I exclaimed. (The Portuguese version of the name *Heidi* is *Aida*, so this is what I am called at home in Mozambique.) There were about forty people in church. Soon everybody started yelling and screaming, "Mama Aida can see!"

Thought for Reflection

Are you willing to press into the promise God has placed in you? Even if its fulfillment seems a long time coming, don't give up or give in. Hold fast to the truth God has called you to.

Prayer

Lord, there are some days when it is hard to hold on to the promises You have given me. Help me to be steadfast, knowing that "He who promised is faithful." I trust You to come through.

DAY 67
CONTINUE TO SAY YES

If you love Me, keep My commandments.
—JOHN 14:15

Sometimes God fulfills His promises to us, but it isn't always in the way we expect. After I received the promise that the blind would see and praying for so long, the first three to be healed were women named "Aida," which is "Heidi" in Portuguese. In three days three blind women with the same name as mine received sight!

When I asked Jesus what this meant, I thought He would say something complimentary. Perhaps He would tell me I was coming into my healing anointing. What I actually felt from the Lord shocked me. I felt Him say I was blind!

I fell apart. I begged God to open my eyes and let me see. He did. In my spirit I suddenly saw the Western and the Eastern bride of Christ—countless outwardly rich churches that are, in truth, badly malnourished. I saw the Father's many, many children in affluent nations trying to live on a few stray crumbs from His table each day. I saw people clothed wealthily on the outside yet spiritually dressed in rags. I saw a secret multitude of the hungry, poor, and naked. I believe Jesus was asking, "Won't you love them too?"

For eighteen years I had barely done any speaking in the West. I was happy to be hidden away in slums and garbage dumps, learning about the kingdom from drug addicts and poor children. To be honest, I didn't much care for most of the Western church. But one day, while praying, I heard the Lord tell me I was to give one-third of my time to ministering in first-world nations.

I started crying. I did not want to go. I could hardly imagine leaving my children for even a third of my time. Then I sensed the Lord reminding me of John 14:15: "If you love Me, you will obey what I command."

"Lord," I wept, "whatever You want, I will do."

I received fulfillment of the promise God

had given to me, but He shook up my life in a different way, a way I had never expected. In these instances, when a curve ball is thrown at you, it is imperative to say yes.

Thought for Reflection

Have you ever thought about what you would do if God asked you to do something outside your desires and comfort zone? Would it be difficult to say yes? Know that God is in the business of stretching us and testing our willingness to obey, so commit today to saying yes regardless.

Prayer

Lord, I want to say yes to You, regardless of what it is You are asking of me. I know that at first I may not want what You want, but I trust that You know what is best. Prepare me to work in areas I have never even dreamed of.

DAY 68
FINDING JOY IN OBEDIENCE

Let us look to Jesus, the author and finisher of our faith, who for the joy that was set before Him endured the cross, despising the shame, and is seated at the right hand of the throne of God.
—HEBREWS 12:2

It had been a long while since I had worked with anyone except the poorest of the poor. I had not ministered in the Western world for many years. I more or less refused to look at the wealthier churches of the world. Now the Lord was opening my eyes and showing me that He wanted to feed fresh bread from heaven to westerners and easterners of all kinds. He wanted to put salve on their eyes too, so they could see clearly.

I began to travel for one-third of the year. I was obedient, but for a long time I was not joyful about it. I often said I hated conferences. When I left Mozambique, I missed my children every moment of every day. While I sat in pleasant hotels, I longed to be with the poor in the dirt. I was constantly homesick.

One day the Lord gently rebuked me. He told me He was glad I obeyed, but He also wanted me to be joyful in the work. This greatly impacted my heart.

I was in Ukraine when the Lord began to teach me how to do what He was asking. I felt He told me to see the one in front of me. At that moment I was holding a Ukrainian lady in my arms, and suddenly, to my amazement, I felt the very same love for that woman as I did for my Mozambican children.

Soon after that I was hugging and praying for an Israeli youth in Jerusalem. All at once I felt the deep weight of God's affection for the youth's nation and people. I found myself thinking that if I had to, I would gladly take a bullet for them. Right there I literally became willing to lay my life down for this young Jewish man.

More and more each day I started to really see the one God was placing in front of me, and then the next, and the next after that. God taught me to do this while I was in richer nations, just as I had learned to do it in poorer ones. From then on I started to find joy in my travels.

I can also truthfully say that it has become one of my greatest joys to travel around the world, even though not long ago it felt like one of my greatest sacrifices. It is a privilege for me to see people all over the earth yielding their lives to Jesus on the altar and saying, "I will go, no matter what the cost! I will run into my destiny and carry God's love to this lost and dying world!" For the joy that is set before me, I say yes every day to the cost of the promises God is birthing through me.

Thought for Reflection

God may one day ask you to do something you would rather not do. Don't dismiss it just because it isn't your preference. God's call is more important than what you prefer, and being obedient to His call may become one of your greatest joys.

Prayer

Lord, even when You are asking something of me I didn't expect, I want to find joy in it. Knowing that my work pleases You is enough to bring joy to me.

DAY 69
LIVE OUT THE "YES"

By faith Sarah herself also received the ability to conceive seed, and she bore a child when she was past the age, because she judged Him faithful who had promised.
—HEBREWS 11:11

When God places a promise inside us, we have to decide to nurture it and believe that it will be accomplished. Every word God has ever given me required me to be patient and tenacious in walking it out. I have had to make choices and decisions that align with His promises. Saying yes to Him is not something I can do once and then forget about it. I have to live out that yes every day of my life.

Mary had to wait nine months for her promise to be birthed. Sometimes we must wait years to see what the Lord has spoken come to pass. During those nine months Mary was carrying her promise alone. Others were interceding in the temple, but they did not have her baby inside their wombs; they did not literally feel the weight of that baby each day. Mary had to go on a long journey to Bethlehem, and after being turned away from every decent room in the city, she had to wait in a stable to birth her baby. It was dark, there were animals around, it did not smell very pleasant, and only Joseph was there to help her. And then there was the pain of the labor itself. This was not a very glamorous way to see the fulfillment of her promise.

There will be moments when we feel the weight of the promises God has placed inside of us, but we see nothing. We experience only a long journey and a dusty, stinky stable. Maybe no one is cheering us on or affirming our faith; we may even feel embarrassed in the presence of others. When I was praying for blind person after blind person with not one person healed, I could have looked at my circumstances and felt ashamed or confused, especially in front of my friends. I could have given up hope and stopped praying, but I would have missed the breakthrough.

Thought for Reflection

If you give up on the promises God has placed in your heart when things get difficult, those promises will likely never be realized. Instead of looking at those difficulties, keep your eyes on Him and His goodness.

Prayer

Lord, I'm not giving up, even when things get tough. I know Your promises are "yes, and amen." Help me to live out my "yes" to You.

DAY 70
PEACE IN THE FACE OF PERSECUTION

Blessed are the peacemakers, for they
shall be called the sons of God.
—MATTHEW 5:9

As we all are fully aware, living out the yes and continuing to follow the Lord is far from easy; but saying yes when things are rough may be even more important than saying yes when things are easy. The children in Mozambique showed me just how hard it can be to say yes to God, and they proved what God can do when we say yes anyway.

There was an occasion when we had to escape our center in Mozambique in the middle of the night so that we would not be killed. At two o'clock in the morning, with a death warrant out for my life, Rolland and I took our two natural-born children and as many other small children as we could fit in our trucks, leaving behind too many because we had no choice. All I could pray was, "God, You have to take care of them. I don't know what to do or where to go."

A group of people who hated us came the next morning to threaten the children who remained at the center. They ordered the children to stop worshipping. But our children defied them! They worshipped, they danced, and they sang, thanking Jesus for everything.

This infuriated this group. They threw rocks at our children and screamed, "You children, if you want food, you will shut your mouths right now! You are not to worship God. If you worship Him, you will die of hunger. We are willing to take over this center if you stop worshipping God. God does not exist. If you read your Bible, if you pray, you will starve to death."

The children looked at them and sang all the louder. The people were infuriated, so they changed what they were saying and promised the children a home, food, and an education if they would deny their faith and stay behind at my old center, which the group had confiscated.

In spite of the temptation, not even one

child stayed. The children responded in the opposite spirit. The children spoke peace to them. The children knew they were true sons and daughters of God, and their Father in heaven would take care of them.

They all took off. All of our children, every one of them, came to us in our little office, singing worship songs in their native Shangaan language.

They truly were peacemakers! They knew God was their Father. They overcame through a love that never fails. Even if their lives had been taken from them, they would never have stopped worshipping Jesus! These were not some famous church leaders. They were children without shoes who had been beaten up and persecuted but who refused to forsake the gospel.

They were told they were just street children—without intelligence, without worth, and without any hope in the world. These children stood up to those leaders who threatened their lives, and they walked in peace.

In the face of evil, our children showed mercy. In the face of hatred, they demonstrated Jesus's kindness. In the midst of persecution, they did not fight back, but they embodied what it means to be a peacemaker. Truly they are the sons and daughters of God.

Thought for Reflection

Have you ever been asked to show mercy in the face of evil, kindness in the face of hatred, or peace in the face of persecution? Doing so is difficult, yes, but it is the way of God. Ask Him today for the strength to be a peacemaker.

Prayer

Lord, it is difficult to follow You and say yes when I am under attack. But I submit the difficult situations to You and ask for Your strength to show mercy and love when I am in the midst of them.

DAY 71
HOLY DESPERATION

*As the deer pants after the water brooks, so
my soul pants after You, O God. My soul
thirsts for God, for the living God.*
—PSALM 42:1–2

The poor have taught me desperation for
God through their hunger. When I think
of desperation, I think of Alberto, who is a
badly crippled and deformed man. One day
my personal assistant, Shara, was driving a
Land Rover full of singing children downtown
in Pemba when she saw Antonio, crawling in
the dust and dirt of the Mozambican streets.
Shara stopped for him and carried him back
to our Bible school.

Before we could build him a mud-hut
house and arrange transportation for him to
come to Bible class, he crawled for hours on
his hands every single day to get there. After
our Mozambican pastors prayed for him, he

gave his life to Jesus. Alberto was carried to the ocean to be baptized. Out from the turquoise waters, Alberto rose with a bright smile beaming ear to ear. Now he brings the gospel wherever he crawls. As Paul wrote, in having nothing, the poor possess all things because they have God.

Through her writings, Mother Teresa helps us to articulate the heart of Jesus to His people:

> Hungry for love, He looks at you.
> Thirsty for kindness, He begs from you.
> Naked for loyalty, He hopes in you.
> Sick and imprisoned for friendship, He wants from you.
> Homeless for shelter in your heart, He asks of you.
> Will you be that one to Him?[1]

We can find the face of God in the poor: "Truly I say to you, as you have done it for one of the least of these brothers of Mine, you have done it for me" (Matt. 25:40). We do what we do only for Him—in Jesus, through Jesus, with Jesus, to Jesus. We make ourselves totally available to Him. What joy to find Him as we give our lives for love!

Thought for Reflection

Have you ever been truly desperate for something? I'm not talking about being simply desirous of having it, as you may be for a new house or car. I mean so desperate that you would give anything, do anything to get it. That's the way we are to be in our longing for God—so hungry and thirsty for Him that nothing else will satisfy. Consider what it will take for you to yearn for Him "as the deer pants after the water brooks."

Prayer

Lord, let me be as desperate as Alberto was to know You. Help me to seek You with everything in me.

PART 8

BELIEVE FOR THE IMPOSSIBLE

DAY 72
BELIEVE FOR THE IMPOSSIBLE

For God is the One working in you, both
to will and to do His good pleasure.
—PHILIPPIANS 2:13

I'm sure most Christians have trouble believing at times that the promises God has given them will come true. But consider Mary's promise again: How unbelievable was that? The first thing Mary said when she heard it was, "How will this be, since I am a virgin?" There was no natural way for her promise to come to pass. Jewish Scripture gave her no reference point for what was happening. It must have seemed utterly impossible.

This is how our promises from the Lord often look: completely and utterly impossible! If your promise does not seem impossible, it is likely not from God.

Naturally speaking, I am completely

wrong for the kind of work I do. I am a white woman from Laguna Beach, which is a prosperous part of California. For Mozambique I am the wrong color and gender, and from the wrong socioeconomic background.

God makes us right for the tasks He asks of us, even when they seem impossible. He is after those who simply remain willing to give all that they are, people who long for full possession by the Holy Spirit.

When the Lord called us to the Makua tribe in Mozambique, there was nothing we could do to make the tribe love Jesus. We could not come up with any kind of realistic plan to make it happen. At first it seemed as if they did not want to know Jesus. That might have been discouraging to us, but we believed God had declared this was their time of visitation. We knew they would meet Him and know Him because of what He alone would do.

A little while before we moved to the northern city of Pemba, we flew up there to visit. We wanted to see where the Lord had asked us to move. As we explored Pemba and the surrounding areas for the first time, we found ourselves trying to get over the shock of being told to go to yet another piece of dirt in the middle of nowhere and start over from nothing. There was little business. Electricity and water were sporadic. There was no Internet access, which was hugely challenging because we handle most of our administration via e-mail. We did not have the financial resources to start a new base. We had no place to live. Starting over felt overwhelming; it felt impossible, as if we weren't the right ones to take on the task. But impossible never stops God.

If you could produce it by your own effort and ability, it would not need to be supernatural. It has to be supernatural to be God. That is who He is—He is supernatural love manifested. By yourself you cannot produce what He wants to birth in you and through you. God is not after spectacular abilities. He is after given hearts and yielded lives.

Thought for Reflection

Do your promises seem impossible? If you are certain they are from God, you can trust that He will fulfill them, no matter how impossible they look to you or how unqualified you think you are. God is not looking for ability; He's looking for availability. Have you made yourself available to Him?

Prayer

Lord, some of the promises You have made to me seem utterly impossible to my human mind. I believe You will fulfill them, anyway. I'm not going to give up because I know You will do as You have said.

BIRTHING THE SUPERNATURAL

But Jesus looked at them and said, "With men this is impossible, but with God all things are possible."
—MATTHEW 19:26

Like many of you, I have felt ill equipped for the work God has called me to. I told Him once how wrong I thought I was for the work He had given me. I felt Him say that was precisely what would allow Him to birth something *supernatural* through me.

Soon after we moved to Pemba, we held an outreach on the outskirts of the town. A crowd showed up, but for a long time nothing worked very well. A well-known preacher had come to visit us and was trying his best to deliver a rousing sermon. No one seemed to be paying much attention. Here and there fights were breaking out. After a while some people began throwing sand and rocks at us.

The service was quickly turning dangerous. As the situation grew worse and worse, God reminded me of what He had said: "*Go and get My lost Makua bride.*"

As I cried out to the Lord, asking Him what I should do, I felt He was leading me to give an altar call for the demonized. Given this crowd—most of whom were of another faith, mixed with the local traditions of witchcraft— that did not sound like a good plan to me. I did it anyway. In my experience, when the Holy Spirit overshadows you, you do strange things. I asked the crowd if they would like to see the power of God, and then I invited everyone who suffered from demonic afflictions to come to the front.

To my surprise about thirty people came forward immediately. As they made their way through the crowd, they started twitching, growling, and manifesting demonic spirits. I was not sure what to do. I had prayed for individuals with demons before, but I had never seen anyone give an altar call for the demonized.

Everyone in that part of Africa knows

something about evil spirits. The crowd was interested now. They looked on eagerly.

Asking God for help, I loudly commanded all the demons to go in Jesus's name. All thirty people fell down immediately. Wherever they fell, they lay stuck to the cement. They could not do anything.

I went down the line and picked them up one by one, asking each of them what happened. All that any of them could tell me was that they were feeling much better. All but two had stopped manifesting. I told those two to wait at one side of the line so I could pray for them again. At a second prayer those two dropped to the pavement again. Every person who had come forward for deliverance was now free.

I then asked the crowd, "Who wants Jesus?"

Many cried, "We do!" Everyone knelt down in the dirt and prayed to receive Him.

Thought for Reflection

God can use you, exactly as you are. In fact, your weaknesses allow His strength to shine through. As 2 Corinthians 12:9 says, His strength is made perfect in weakness. Yield to Him and allow His light to shine through. Allow Him to birth the supernatural through you.

Prayer

Lord, I don't always understand how, but I believe You can use me. Shape me and mold me into the person You want me to be.

DAY 74
TRUST THE HOLY SPIRIT

But the Counselor, the Holy Spirit, whom the Father will send in My name, will teach you every-thing and remind you of all that I told you.
—JOHN 14:25–26

Have you ever had to rely so fully on the Holy Spirit to work in a situation that with-out Him, you know nothing would be accomplished? In our ministry we have been in such a situation many times, one in which utter dependence on Him is our only path forward.

A few years ago the Lord stirred me up to reach the most isolated people in Cabo Delgado—the ones living in scattered coastal villages along the region's many islands and inlets. Most are unreachable by road. They had never heard the gospel. As soon as I learned about them, I began to intercede for them daily. Eventually our ministry was able to buy a small boat we took to a village called Londo.

When Pastor Jose, Dilo (my adopted son), and I arrived at the village, we asked who knew the chief. In Mozambique you do not enter a village without getting permission from the chief. They said he was on a long fishing trip, but that the man next in charge would talk to us. We hiked up a muddy hill and found this person in an old carpenter's shed.

The man gave us permission to speak to the villagers, who slowly gathered around us as we started to sing hymns in Makua. When most of the village had arrived, we told them about the man named Jesus who healed the sick, cast out evil spirits, and loved them without condition. They said they would like to meet Him. In fact, they wanted us to bring Jesus along on our boat next time we visited.

I shared how Jesus had died to take away their sins and had then risen from the dead. I told them that now Jesus lived inside my heart, in the hearts of Jose and Dilo, and in everyone who was willing to believe.

We played an audio recording of the Gospel of John read in Makua for the villagers.

They asked many questions. Before the sun went down, they all invited Jesus to live in their hearts.

They asked us to come back as soon as we could to tell them more, but on our way home one of the boat's engines blew up. We made it home at a crawl, but it took six weeks, a parts shipment from Canada, and a Filipino mechanic to get the engine running again.

Six weeks is a long time for new believers to go without guidance. But we were leaving them in the trustworthy hands of the Holy Spirit.

When we finally came back, the villagers saw the boat approaching in the distance. They lined up on the shore, singing and dancing. They were quoting scriptures and singing songs they had memorized from the solar-powered audio Bibles we had left them. It was as if the parable of the sower had come to life: "He who received seed on the good ground is he who hears the word and understands it, who indeed bears fruit" (Matt. 13:23). Trusting in the Holy Spirit was, indeed, the best thing we could do for this village.

Thought for Reflection

Think about a time when you've been in a situation in which utter dependence on the Holy Spirit was your only option. How did He resolve the situation? Do you now have faith to believe the Lord will work in miraculous ways when you rely on and trust in Him?

Prayer

Holy Spirit, I want to see miracles! Help me to rely on You in every situation that seems hopeless and trust that You will resolve each one supernaturally. Nothing is impossible for You.

DAY 75
THE IMPORTANCE
OF PRAYER

Be anxious for nothing, but in everything, by prayer and supplication with gratitude, make your requests known to God. And the peace of God, which surpasses all understanding, will protect your hearts and minds through Christ Jesus.
—PHILIPPIANS 4:6–7

If you have served in ministry very long, you know how difficult it can be. If you are just stepping into ministry, just beginning to see the fulfillment of promises God has given you, you will soon face various trials and attacks from the enemy. When such trials and attacks come, pray. Pray intently, and ask those who love you and love the Lord to pray as well.

One night a fierce storm rose up just as we were arriving at the village of Londo on our boat. We put out in our dinghy and got tossed everywhere by the surf. Before we made it to the shore, we were scared for our lives. We were sopping wet. As usual the villagers were waiting for us on the sand. They were especially excited to see us this time. They wanted to show me my new home. They had made me a fabulous new mud hut on a hill near the church and school we had helped them build.

Their gift was overwhelming. I was laughing and hugging them when I got a call from the boat captain. He was shouting something about the boat sinking.

"No! Not now!" I yelled into the radio. I was busy enjoying my hut.

"You might not want to hear it, but we're sinking!" the captain yelled back.

There was no choice but for a rescue boat to come from Pemba and pick us up. Unfortunately our captain was inexperienced, and the rescue boat's captain was drunk. Our captain shot his single emergency flare sideways into the water. It took the rescuers hours to find our vessel. The weather was worsening, and their crew was infuriated. They picked up the people who were on our sinking boat and left those of us on shore—Jose, Dilo, Mario, and me—behind.

The villagers shrugged and built us a fire. I laughed to myself while thinking of the apostle Paul's trials. Stoned? Check. Beaten? Check. Jailed? Check. Hungry and cold? Check. Shipwrecked? Check!

Before going to bed, I climbed the biggest termite hill in the village, hoping to find cell phone reception from across the bay in Pemba. I got one bar. In the few minutes before my battery died, I texted a team of intercessors at our base, asking for prayer for a miracle. This is the most critical kind of support there is. If your dreams are from God, they will always need intercession. Like midwives, praying people help birth the miraculous promises in your life. They will make the obstacles before you more bearable by soliciting God's help.

Thought for Reflection

Are you surrounded by prayer warriors and intercessors? As you step more fully into the promise God has for you, having a prayer covering will become more and more necessary. Find friends you can trust to pray for you, and commit to praying for them, as well.

Prayer

Lord, teach me how to pray without ceasing. Cause my trust in You to grow. I want to know that I can call on You in times of trial so that I will be able to move forward in the work You have called me to do.

Day 76
Paying the Price for Your Promise

I have become all things to all men, that I might by all means save some. This I do for the gospel's sake, that I might partake of it with you. Do you not know that all those who run in a race run, but one receives the prize? So run, that you may obtain it….So, therefore, I run, not with uncertainty. So I fight, not as one who beats the air.
—1 Corinthians 9:22–24, 26

Have you ever been shocked at the price of groceries at the store? What about gas at the gas pump? Prices seem to rise ever higher, but we buy food and gas anyway. Even when the cost is exorbitant, it is worth it to have milk and bread and eggs for our children or gas to get to work. How much more will it be worth it to pay whatever price is required to see our promises from God fulfilled?

After being left in Londo when our boat

sank, Mario fired up the dinghy, trying to get us home. As it turned out, we had made a bad mistake. The dinghy leaked. Soon we were knee-deep in water. We thought we were prepared, but as the water kept rising, we realized we were all in serious trouble. Life vests would not save us if we were swept out to sea. In earnest now, we prayed for God to send a rescuer.

Jose could not swim. Going on our boat always made him nervous. He went anyway. He said he would do anything for Jesus. Now he was getting to prove it.

Each of us had things we needed to do; we weren't done living yet. Pastor Jose's wife was nine months pregnant. For the last ten years Jose had prayed for a baby. Knee-deep in rising water, Jose cried out, "I just want to see my baby born!" Dilo was dreaming about food. Mario, our assistant skipper, had no dreams to discuss. I heard from God that I would preach the gospel in universities around the world. I had been scheduled to fly to Oxford, England, to speak at an event called Love Oxford the next day. How would I give birth to my promise?

We saw a small vessel in the distance. As it

came closer, we saw it was an ancient-looking fishing boat. We whistled madly and flailed our arms. It came to us crewed by an old man. He offered to take us back to Pemba—for an exorbitant fee. I was furious that he would try to take advantage of us with the water reaching our waists. I told him I would never pay him so much. He promptly revved up his engine, happy to leave us there.

My brothers started laughing and crying. They wailed and prayed aloud for God to give me a brain. I realized I needed to call our rescuer back and give him whatever he wanted. I had to go and preach at Oxford. Pastor Jose had to see his baby being born. Dilo had to eat. Mario just needed to care. I would pay any price to see God's promises birthed in our lives—to bring the love of Jesus to the most hidden people groups, to the top universities, to the lost, the broken, and the dying. I would pay anything to see a mighty movement of radical, laid-down lovers released into every corner of the earth. I supposed I could pay this price too.

After agreeing to hand over a small fortune, we climbed into the fisherman's boat.

Thought for Reflection

It seems ridiculous to have to pay to be rescued; that was the cost, however, of seeing our dreams fulfilled. Someday you may be asked to pay a price that will in some way lead to promises being fulfilled. In this moment, remember what your promise from God is worth. Think of the lost that will be reached, the hungry fed, and the lonely loved.

Prayer

Lord, help me to remember what I'm receiving when I'm asked to pay a high price. Put it in perspective so I know that the fulfillment of Your promises is more important than whatever it is I must give up.

DAY 77
DON'T TAKE OFFENSE

He who is void of wisdom despises his neigh-
bor, but a man of understanding holds his peace.
—PROVERBS 11:12

When you are in ministry, it is important to guard your heart from offense. I once
made the mistake of taking offense too easily,
and my response nearly kept me from being
able to bless a group of men who had rescued
my friends and me.

We were in a broken-down boat being
pushed toward jagged black rocks sticking
out from the water. We prayed intensely in
the Spirit. We prayed for our lives and for
the miraculous promises God had placed in
us. Everything looked lost when in the distance we spotted a local wooden fishing boat.
The fishermen paddled over.

The first thing I noticed was that the

fishermen were naked. They had not expected to find anyone else on the ocean that day.

Covering my eyes, I asked if they could help us.

Right away one of them jumped into the ocean and started heading for the shore. He was a powerful swimmer, but at first I had no idea why he had gone into the water. As he was swimming to shore, another fisherman helped a man to safety who had previously tried unsuccessfully to rescue us.

The fisherman who jumped off the boat came swimming back with shorts for himself and the other five fishermen. They covered up and helped us onto their boat. In my life I have been honored in many ways. I have been put in seven-star hotels. I have been taken to extraordinary banquets. On occasion I have flown in private planes and helicopters. However, I had never been honored as much as I was by these men.

When we were nearly back to our side of the bay, I remembered I had a copy of the New Testament in my waist pack. I also remembered the day when the local representative of a large Bible society explained to me that the organization wanted to donate thirty thousand New Testament books to Iris Global. These Bibles came with a condition, however. Although I, a woman, was one of the senior leaders of Iris, the Bible society did not want any of their New Testaments to be given to a woman. Only Mozambican men were to receive them.

At first I was offended. Then the Holy Spirit reminded me that there were hundreds of men in our region working with Iris who were ready to receive this priceless gift and to distribute it to others. That very day I called over one hundred men to our office to receive the first of these New Testaments. I waited on the sidelines while they took them—and in the end, one of the men made sure to give me a few of the extra copies as he left. I still had the last one of these with me.

When we reached our side of the bay, I took out this little New Testament and read John 3:16 to my rescuers. I was surprised to discover that one of the fishermen knew how to read. I left the book with him. All six men received the Lord Jesus as their Savior on the shore before we said good-bye.

Thought for Reflection

If you want to birth the miraculous, you cannot afford to get offended. Offense prevents you from carrying the promise to full term, and you never know how God will turn an offensive situation into good for you or others.

Prayer

Lord, guard my heart from those who wish to hurt me. Don't let their comments or actions distract me from following Your call on my life or cloud my understanding of what You are asking me to do.

DAY 78
A HARD-WON HARVEST

*Blessed is the man who remains stead-
fast under trial, for when he has stood the
test he will receive the crown of life, which
God has promised to those who love him.*
—JAMES 1:12, ESV

As all humans are aware, trials are a part of life. Trials in ministry may be even more common. But at one point I felt as if I had faced too many of them, one right after the other: our boat sank while we were in the village of Londo, our dingy sank while Jose, Dilo, Mario, and I were trying to return home, and our rescue was costly. But I persevered and saw one of God's promises begin to be fulfilled in my life.

When I finally returned home after being rescued at sea, I was ready to birth the promise I had been thinking and praying about: preaching at universities across the world. I arrived home wet, hungry, and completely exhausted. Regardless, the first thing I had to do was pack for my trip to Oxford.

The following day I flew to Johannesburg, the capital of South Africa, and then got in line for my next flight to England. I found out my seat was in the middle row in the very back of the plane. I was still far from properly rested. The thought of being stuck between three other passengers for the nine-hour flight made me want to cry. I asked the flight agents if I could possibly wait to board the plane until the last moment, in case any aisle seats became available. I was flying on an airline I did not normally use. I did not expect much favor. I waited, praying, as the other passengers boarded, feeling frayed and stretched to my limit.

Just before they closed the doors, they called me to the gate desk. The attendant smiled and said, "We have an aisle seat for you. It's in first class."

I burst into tears.

After I reached my seat, they gave me a set of pajamas. I had never experienced such an incredibly comfortable flight before in my life. I slept all the way to London.

I arrived at Oxford in traditional British weather—cold, heavy rain. The event was outdoors. As we worshipped together, the presence of God seemed to fill the outdoor area so that no one paid any attention to the downpour. I saw countless men and women bowing their knees under their umbrellas. Many made commitments to carry their own miraculous promises to full term, no matter the cost. Some fell facedown in the mud, floored under the weight of God's presence. All at once everything I had been through over the last several days felt utterly worthwhile.

Thought for Reflection

Trials come, but persevere through them. Hold on to God's promise. You will see it come forth, and everything you went through to receive it will be worth the price you paid.

Prayer

Lord, I know I will face trials. I ask You to be with me through them and *to encourage me when I don't want to go on. Help me to make them count by using them to make a difference for Your kingdom.*

Day 79
Cast Your Bread Upon the Waters

They sold their property and goods and distributed them to all, according to their need.
—ACTS 2:45

Sacrificial giving is an essential part of our lives as Christians. God calls us to give to others as they have need, even when it is not easy or convenient for us to do so.

After our boat sank, we were able to purchase a yacht for less than 10 percent of its original worth and restore it. We named it *Iris Compassion* and let the captain decide where to go for our first voyage. The captain knew of a village we had never visited before and took us there while we worshipped on the sunny deck.

As usual we intended to go and find the chief before doing anything else. But before we could go exploring, we saw a little boat motoring in from the open bay. Those aboard waved as they headed past us toward the village. We asked them to stop for a moment so we could throw them a big bag of fresh bread. We tossed it to their boat, but it fell short, landing in the water. The plastic was well sealed, though, and the bread stayed afloat.

As they came around to pick up the bread, the Lord reminded me of the scripture, "Cast your bread upon the waters, for you will find it after many days" (Eccles. 11:1). As they got closer, I asked them in their language if they knew where the local chief was. The man in the middle looked up and said, "I am the chief." Right away he offered to take me on a tour of his village.

At that moment the engine on the chief's boat choked, sputtered, and died. (We seem to have quite the anointing for engines at Iris Global!) We were happy to help and sent our mechanic to examine the problem. They needed a specific kind of spark plug that we happened to have on board. I asked our captain to give them one. He looked at me quite strangely. Spare parts can be very hard to come by in Mozambique, and we were likely to need everything we had brought with us to keep the *Iris Compassion* going, but I insisted.

If we are to carry our promises to full term, we need to help others do the same. If we want to arrive at our intended destinations, we must help others cross the water. We all have things that our brothers and sisters need in order to fulfill their own destinies. We are called to share and provide those things.

In the village we received a warmer welcome than we ever had before. Hundreds of villagers gathered, and the chief asked us why we had come. I started with John 3:16. After I shared, everyone who could hear us bowed his head and received Jesus as Lord and Savior. All those present gave themselves to Jesus without question.

We didn't give the spark plug to the chief so he would welcome us or listen to our explanation of Christ, but I believe our generosity helped to open his heart.

Thought for Reflection

Do you consider yourself a giver? Are you able to be generous even when doing so requires a sacrifice?

Prayer

Lord, I know that You are a giver, and I want to be like You. Please help me to become one who is always ready to share whatever I have with those in need.

DAY 80
NEVER GIVE UP

But thanks be to God, who gives us the victory through our Lord Jesus Christ! Therefore, my beloved brothers, be steadfast, unmovable, always abounding in the work of the Lord, knowing that your labor in the Lord is not in vain.
—1 CORINTHIANS 15:57–58

Sometimes we feel foolish dreaming the sorts of dreams God puts in our hearts. Our truest dreams always look too big for us. We may be afraid of how bizarre we will look trying to achieve them. We might start out with a lofty goal such as paddling a kayak alone to islands many miles away—a feat I attempted before we were able to purchase our first boat—only to find the task is much harder than we ever knew. Nonetheless, we can be confident that God will "fulfill His purpose for [us]" (Ps. 138:8).

Scripture tells us that Paul prayed for the

church to have patience and endurance (Col. 1:11). Sometimes we give up too quickly. I might have given up when my kayak idea turned out to be laughably inadequate. I might have given up when our first real boat sank and we found ourselves shipwrecked.

Never mind the boats—I might have given up on Mozambique in general many times before that. I might have given up when people shot at me or when gangs were chasing me. I might have given up when we were in deep psychological distress after friends of ours in the Congo were dismembered in a church with machetes. I might have given up when I was reported in the newspapers to be a drug dealer because of mistaken results at a lab, where they were testing some vitamins that were donated to us. I might have given up on the fifth, sixth, or seventh occasion when crowds began to stone me for preaching about Jesus.

Most especially I might have given up when my husband, Rolland, got cerebral malaria and suffered a series of micro strokes that almost killed him. Though he was eventually healed, for two years he lost his short-term memory and was totally unable to function in ministry or administration.

The only reason I did not give up at any of these times was because I know the One who placed His promises within me. When you know Him intimately, you never give up, because He is worthy!

Thought for Reflection

Stay steadfast and faithful to the promises the Lord has given you. Don't give up when there are trials. The Lord will take care of you and bring you through. He will fulfill His purpose for you.

Prayer

Lord, there are times I am tempted to give up. When I haven't yet seen fruit and circumstances are difficult, I struggle to hold on to Your promises. Help me through these times, please. I want to be faithful to Your call.

DAY 81
THE GOD OF THE IMPOSSIBLE

Jesus, looking at them, said, "With men it is impossible, but not with God. For with God all things are possible."
—MARK 10:27

I imagine you've been concerned at times about how the promises God has given you will be manifest in your life. That's probably because they are so big! God loves to promise things beyond what we think are possible because He knows we will have to depend on Him for their fulfillment. What is impossible for us to accomplish in our own strength and with our own ability or ingenuity is possible for Him.

When the Lord stirred me up to reach the most isolated people in Cabo Delgado—the ones living in scattered coastal villages along the region's many islands and inlets—I was tempted to feel as if it was impossible. How were we supposed to get there? Most of the villages are unreachable by road, and we had problem after problem with our boats. But I knew these people had never heard the gospel, and I was determined to try. I was faithful to the promise the Lord had given me, no matter how impossible it seemed—and He was faithful to fulfill it.

The Lord wants to take you beyond who you are and what you can do. He is the One who can take a barren woman in her old age, as He did Mary's cousin Elizabeth, and make her fruitful for the first time. Imagine Mary's surprise when an angel told her: "Listen, your cousin Elizabeth has also conceived a son in her old age. And this is the sixth month with her who was declared barren. For with God nothing will be impossible" (Luke 1:36–37).

As God's children we should be seeking for Him to overshadow us. Two things will come from being overshadowed. The first is a particular promise from God that is naturally impossible to fulfill. The second is a general promise from God that *nothing* is impossible with Him.

Our God is the God of the impossible. He can take a barren ministry and breathe His

Spirit into it. Even in your old age He can breathe over you and cause you to bear a ministry, a promise, or a revelation—a beautiful gift that will carry His glory to the ends of the earth. He can take the most barren and broken life—even the kind of life that has aborted its own promises many times over—and in it plant a glorious new promise, along with all the strength that is needed to carry it to full term.

Thought for Reflection

Have you examined your promise from God and deemed it impossible? Don't give up! Nothing is too big for God, and He does not lie. He will fulfill the promise He gave you.

Prayer

Lord, You are the God of the impossible. I believe You can do exceedingly, abundantly beyond anything I think, ask, or imagine. Show up in my life; bring the impossible to fruition.

PART 9

ENTER INTO HIS REST

DAY 82
ENTER INTO HIS REST

Therefore, since the promise of entering His rest remains, let us fear lest any of you should seem to come short of it. For the gospel was preached to us as well as to them. But the word preached did not benefit them, because it was not mixed with faith in those who heard it. For we who have believed have entered this rest, as He has said, "As I have sworn in My wrath, 'They shall not enter My rest.'" However, His works have been finished since the creation of the world.

—HEBREWS 4:1–3

Do you find it difficult to rest? Are you always working or engaging in some type of ministry activity? As you step into the promise God has for you, remember how important rest is.

There is a place of rest in the heart of God. In this place we learn to trust Him in the midst of chaos and difficulties. As we lean upon Him and hear His heartbeat, we discover its rhythm—when to run, when to rest, and when to release. As we contend to enter into the rest He has prepared for us, we ourselves become resting places where He can come and dwell in greater fullness.

We can enter into the storms of life and release love only when we have learned how to rest in God. Hebrews 4:1–3 tells us to be careful not to fall short of His rest. Also, we will not achieve rest through the merits of our works, so that no one should boast. (See Ephesians 2:9.) Rather, we need to rest in the promises of God. We will be safe in the King's arms. Indeed, we must learn to live there.

Many things in my life threaten to steal my rest. Once, when I was particularly exhausted from a busy week, I decided it was time to make a promise to my young assistant that I would model rest for her generation. I told her I would change my schedule and cut back. I told her I would do less so I could spend more time in God's presence.

Sometimes it is a difficult promise to keep, but it burned in my heart as I made it.

Around that same time two of my watches

malfunctioned in two days. The first watch, a very reliable model, stopped for no apparent reason. I bought another cheaper one at the airport. The same thing happened to that one the next day. I believe God was showing me that if I would trust Him and do less, He would do more.

I admit that I am not always very good at this, but God keeps challenging me to go deeper and trust in His control. He encourages me that if we will take time to rest in Him, He will do more with our lives than we could ever hope to achieve otherwise.

Thought for Reflection

Resting in the Lord has a lot to do with trust. Are you able to find peace in His presence while You trust Him to work on your behalf, or do you feel as if nothing will be accomplished during your time with Him?

Prayer

Lord, it seems as if there is always more and more work to be done. I want to press into Your rest during busy times because

I know I need it in order to accomplish all You have for me to do. Help me to learn when to push forward and when to pull away with You.

DAY 83
SABBATH REST

Therefore a rest remains for the people of God.
For whoever enters His rest will also cease
from his own works, as God did from His.
—HEBREWS 4:9–10

During biblical times God reminded His people over and over again to "remember the Sabbath" and "keep the Sabbath." (See Exodus 20:8; 31:13–16; Leviticus 19:3, 30, for example.) He intended for them to observe the Sabbath as a holy day of rest on which no work was to be done. Though you would not know it to look at our culture, in which stores, restaurants, and other establishments are open seven days a week, His command is applicable to us today.

Sadly, when told that they absolutely must rest, many believers become frantic. "We need to go!" they say. "We need to run!" Often I am this sort of person myself.

Yes, we do need to run—but we also need to rest. This is part of the rhythm of God's heart. God has given a Sabbath rest for the people of God. Anyone who enters this rest also rests from his or her own work just as God did. God worked six days, and He rested on the seventh.

Of course, we do not just lie on the floor resting seven days a week. We would be sore and tired from resting! At the same time, if we never rest, then we will never run. We cannot make it through our marathon without times of refreshing.

No can be an anointed word. We cannot be saviors to all. We are servants, daughters, sons, and brides, but not saviors. There is only one Savior. We cannot have His job.

We are called and allowed to rest. God is able to keep His world going, and in the meantime it is very important that we do not do more than He is asking.

Some of us think the principle of rest does not apply to us. I assure you—it really does! We have to rest, beloved of God. You are going to get more accomplished through resting than through striving. It is important to take a Sabbath.

I try to pray for three to five hours every day. I get up early. I pray and I worship, and then I pray some more. Once I thought that could count as my Sabbath somehow, but later I found out God did not agree. He also wants me to play.

It was amazing to discover that God likes to stop and play. He told me one time to fly all of our senior leaders from the various nations in which Iris Global operates to Pemba. We were to play and pray. I asked if we could strategize as well. He said no!

We gathered on the *Iris Compassion* and drifted out to sea. We played and prayed—and ate! It might sound worthless in the natural, but God loved it. Some of us are so driven that we need to be very deliberate about learning to play—but I believe that if we learn how to play with our leaders and our friends, we will work together a lot better in the days to come.

Thought for Reflection

God has commanded you to rest. This does not mean He wants you to be lazy, but He understands our human frame and knows that we need a balance of work, rest, and play in our lives. Make a plan today for how you can incorporate all these into your week.

Prayer

Lord, help me to see the good that rest can do for my soul, and give me the peace of mind to take a step back from work. Teach me to work, rest, and play in proper balance.

DAY 84
RESTING IN THE RIDE

*Let us labor therefore to enter that rest, lest
anyone fall by the same pattern of unbelief.*
—HEBREWS 4:11

It is often a struggle to find time to rest.
Part of the reason is that there are so many
demands on us due to family, work, and ministry responsibilities and we find it difficult to
pull away. I have an issue with that too.

I am incredibly tenacious. I know how to
put in eighteen-hour workdays for many days
at a time. I pushed hard through ten years
of university to complete a PhD in systematic theology. I understand what it means to
labor diligently.

I share these parts of my background so
that you will not be tempted to think rest
comes easily for me. But despite my personality, I have come to understand that we are
commissioned to make every effort to enter

324

rest. This may sound strange, but I grasp what it means because of how much warfare and contending it requires for me to secure a day off. It is much harder than fighting the curses of witch doctors. I am constantly asked to do just one more meeting or one more conference. It is not a simple thing for me to say no, but I do it for the sake of obedience.

I was once coerced into leading a meeting on one of those few days I was supposed to have off. I was exhausted and agitated. Nonetheless, Jesus came to the meeting. I could feel His presence strongly. Suddenly I had a vision. I saw myself sitting on a white horse. I love horses, but I was afraid because this white horse was galloping extremely fast.

I knew this was a picture of my life. It was an image of rapid revival and growth, of all the things I had seen birthed. I remember feeling sure I was going to fall from the horse. But then I sensed His voice saying, "Lean, Heidi, lean!"

I leaned in low over the horse's mane, and there was Jesus behind me, holding me in His arms. As I leaned, I was completely swallowed up inside His heart. We rode as one.

My concern over losing my precious day off dissipated into incredible joy. God had set me up. He did this because He wanted to show Himself strong in the midst of my fatigue and limitation. Once again He taught me it is all about Him.

God wants to take you into a greater place of rest. He wants to bring you to the place where you can continue to ride the white horse even as you lean completely into Him, resting safe and calm in the midst of storms, revivals, and all manner of great works.

Thought for Reflection

Sometimes we must learn to rest in the midst of our work by leaning more heavily on the all-sufficient, all-powerful One. What will it take for you to "let go and let God"?

Prayer

Lord, there are times when taking a day off is simply impossible. Let these times be few, but when they come, teach me how to rest in Your embrace and let You do the work.

DAY 85
REST, RUN, RELEASE

Since then we have a great High Priest who has passed into the heavens, Jesus the Son of God, let us hold firmly to our confession. For we do not have a High Priest who cannot sympathize with our weaknesses, but One who was in every sense tempted like we are, yet without sin. Let us then come with confidence to the throne of grace, that we may obtain mercy and find grace to help in time of need.
—HEBREWS 4:14–16

Jesus made a way for us to "come with confidence" to God's throne when we need grace to help us in times of need. It is in this place that God gives us strategies for how to handle the trials that come our way so we can find rest in spite of them.

We have seen incredible disasters in Mozambique. In one of the worst disasters three hundred fifty of our churches were destroyed by floodwaters.

Even at times like these some rest is important. The only way I know how to rest in such a disaster is to lean in and listen to the heart of God. In the rhythm of God's heart there is resting, there is running, and there is releasing.

When I found out about that particular flood, I was at a conference in Canada. One of my Mozambican sons called me on the phone. He was terribly distraught and said it was one of the worst tragedies he had ever seen—and he had seen a lot. I had no idea how to rest with my son screaming, but I felt the Lord asking me to trust Him and rest in the boat without fear.

God reminded me of the rhythm of run, rest, and release. As I continued to pray and listen, I heard Him saying it was now time to release my sons and daughters.

I started to call our Mozambican sons. Almost all of them had been homeless when we found them. Some had been thieves and bandits, but now they were all grown up and strong in the Lord. We released large sums of money into their hands so they could go and feed the hungry in the refugee camps. We released the keys to our trucks. I was astonished at how responsibly they handled the crisis.

Before long the president, the governor, and the news media had interviewed our team of young Mozambican men and women. It was especially wonderful for me, as a mama, to hide in the back and watch as they shined.

If we will learn the rhythm of God's heart, we will not be afraid to release sons and daughters before they themselves know how they will be able to finish the race. God Himself will ignite their passion. They are going to run far ahead, and we will catch up breathlessly.

There are hundreds and thousands of people doing good and important things for God. No one is supposed to try to do it all. If we do not get into the rhythm of God's heart, we can forget this. We become overwhelmed and get burned out. Being good releasers enables us to rest instead. We have to release life, release the Holy Spirit, release anointing, release leadership, and release people into their many diverse destinies.

Thought for Reflection

Is letting go difficult for you? If so, learn today how to lean into Jesus. Let Him hold you close until you can hear the rhythm of His heartbeat. Then you will know when to rest, when to run, and when to release.

Prayer

Lord, sometimes it is difficult to let go. It is difficult to move aside so others can begin to step into ministry or handle what I am accustomed to handling, whether at home, at work, or in Your service. Give me the courage to take a step back, find rest, and allow others to take my place, and give me the discernment to know when this needs to happen.

DAY 86
BECOME A RESTING PLACE

What? Do you not know that your body is the temple of the Holy Spirit, who is in you, whom you have received from God, and that you are not your own?
—1 CORINTHIANS 6:19

It is important to take time for physical rest. It is equally important to allow the Holy Spirit to indwell and rest in us. We need to learn how to become a resting place for Him. We need to become a temple where God is always invited to come and pour His oil into our lives. Cars without oil, even if they have gas in them, will not function. They need a steady supply of clean, fresh oil in order to move properly.

I could write thousands of pages about the need to take in the harvest or about God's healing glory, but unless we have a continuous provision of heaven's oil, we will never complete God's full calling. The good news is that at all times God is ready to pour it freely over all who desire it.

I was reminded of this truth while lying in the hospital during a season of life when I was very ill. It was 2005, and I had been confined to a hospital in South Africa for over a month with a severe MRSA infection, which is a particularly robust kind of staph infection. I was literally dying. I took it as a lengthy opportunity for constant prayer and worship. I tried to focus on staying filled with the oil of the Holy Spirit.

This was one of the rare times I did not have people lining up to speak with me. A few of the nurses came in for prayer, but that was all. I was glad to pray with them. I remember that they said they felt so much life in my room. I think it is interesting that even while I was dying, there was still palpable life in my room. God is so good that He fills us with the oil of the Holy Spirit even when our bodies fade. In truth, we are genuinely alive only when the oil of His glory-love is filling us up inside.

It is ironic that I was reminded of a necessity of the Christian life while I lay dying. The reminder, though, that true life comes from the indwelling of His Spirit and not from breath in our lungs was an important one for me. We must rest, and we must allow Him to rest in us.

Thought for Reflection

Take a moment to think about the reality of being the temple of the Holy Spirit. What does it mean to have Him dwelling within? How does His presence empower you to fulfill your calling? Are you allowing Him to pour the oil of His anointing over you?

Do you have space in your life for the Spirit to rest in? Do you welcome Him in? Create an inviting environment for the Spirit to rest in.

Prayer

Lord, cleanse my temple so that the Holy Spirit will find a proper resting place. Help me to be aware of His presence and eager to receive all He offers to prepare me for the work You have for me to do.

DAY 87
REMIND GOD OF HIS PROMISES

This I recall to my mind, therefore I have hope.
Through the LORD's mercies we are not con-
sumed, because His compassions fail not. They are
new every morning; great is Your faithfulness.
—LAMENTATIONS 3:21–23, NKJV

Sometimes after God gives us a promise, we find ourselves facing a situation that makes it seem as if the promise can never be fulfilled. This was the case for Abraham, who waited twenty-five years to have a child with his wife, Sarah, after God had told him he would be the father of many nations. He was already seventy-five at the time the promise was given, a time when most men do not consider father-ing a child a physical possibility. By age ninety-nine, the chances of Abraham's being virile were slim. Yet God was faithful to His word, and Sarah conceived and gave birth to Isaac when Abraham was one hundred years old.

There was a time it would have been easy for me to give up on God's promises. I was in the hospital dying of MRSA, a serious staph infection. But while I was there, the Lord spoke to me as I was meditating on the Book of Zechariah. I noticed that the name *Zechariah* actually means "the Lord remembers."

After one doctor came and said I could write my own tombstone, I began to remind God of all His words to me. I reminded Him of His promise that we would take in a million children. I might be ninety-nine years old by the time we have that many, but I will see it accomplished.

I believe God likes His children to remind Him of His promises. Of course, He remembers all His covenants, but when we are able to speak out in faith concerning them, it gladdens His heart.

I told God I was ready to die but that I did not want to die from a flesh-eating disease. I wanted to keep sharing the gospel and ministering until the day Jesus took me home. I called upon His promises to me and feasted on what He revealed through the witness of Zechariah.

Still confined to my bed, I asked Rolland to buy me a new pair of running shoes. Rolland didn't tell me that I was a silly woman for requesting sneakers instead of hospital slippers. He drove right out and went to two different malls to find me the perfect pair. They sat by my bed for weeks. I looked at them every day. I couldn't wait to run. As sick and tired as I was, I had hope because I believed God had a destiny for me.

In Zechariah's day the people were exhausted from building the temple. They were so tired that they had stopped partway. God called for them to return to Him. He asked them to finish His house because He wanted to have mercy on them (Zech. 1:3).

Many of us have been in revival and renewal. We have seen the mighty things of God. There was a time when we were filled to overflowing, but then we grew tired. Sometimes we break down and stop building the things God called us to build.

Through His prophet God is asking us to finish what we have started. God began a mighty work in each of us. He is inviting us to participate in His divine nature. It requires all of us—all our lives and all our years.

Thought for Reflection

When life gets rough, remember the promises God has given you. Remind Him of those promises. Have faith that they will come true, no matter the circumstances you find yourself in.

Prayer

Lord, there are days when I despair of Your promises ever coming true. At those times help me to remind You of them and to grow in faith as I recall Your faithfulness to Your servants. Strengthen me to finish the work You began through me.

DAY 88
GOD IS REBUILDING
HIS HOUSE

Do you not know that you are the temple of
God, and that the Spirit of God dwells in you?
—1 CORINTHIANS 3:16

Where I live in Mozambique, the concept of a house is very different from what it is in the Western world. Instead of residing in a two-story traditional or a contemporary ranch, many of the people live in mud huts. Nevertheless, we all understand the purpose of a house from a natural perspective.

How does our understanding translate from the natural to the spiritual realm?

God spoke to me about houses during the time of my illness. He showed me that my house—my body—had prophetic significance. I had a flesh-consuming disease that was trying to destroy my body. It was eating away stubbornly at my life and skin. It poisoned my system. There are things in the church also that eat away the life of the community and cause it to become weak.

God wants to fully inhabit His house. He wants His people to finish that which He has given them to do. He wants them to be full of life and power as they finish the task.

I reminded the Lord that I loved Him and that I had given my life for ministry. I had served Him day and night for thirty years. I asked Him what the purpose was in my suffering. I had seen Him cure blindness, deafness, and many diseases. Why had I not been healed?

I was fighting the good fight, but I was desperate. I felt that God showed me there is a spiritual fight we are waging together; its outcome determines whether or not we stay full of the Spirit. Finishing our task involves warfare. Sometimes we must accept its trials. I told the Lord to have His will and to make me a resting place for the Holy Spirit.

As difficult as that time was, the Lord was also very kind to me. A white dove fluttered outside my window every morning. It would come back in the cool of the evening and sleep there next to my window. It blessed me deeply because I knew God was speaking. He was asking if I would allow myself to be a resting place for His Spirit.

Of course I wanted to be.

Through Zechariah, God speaks about building His house. You are His house. You are the place where the Holy Spirit dwells. (See 1 Corinthians 3:16; 6:19.) God is rebuilding His house and His people. He is expanding our hearts to carry more of His love.

Thought for Reflection

Do you see your body as the house of the Lord? Are you willing to allow God to make it into a place where the Spirit is pleased to dwell?

Prayer

Lord, I want my body to be a temple, a house for Your Spirit. Do the work necessary to make me into a place You want to dwell.

HOPE AGAINST HOPE

*Against all hope, he believed in hope.... He
did not waver at the promise of God through
unbelief, but was strong in faith, giving glory
to God, and being fully persuaded that what
God had promised, He was able to perform.*
—ROMANS 4:18, 20–21

Sometimes we must step out in faith to do
what God tells us to do even when it doesn't
make sense. Holding our promises in our
hearts, we must forge ahead, believing that
God is able to bring to pass all that He said
He would.

On my thirty-second day in the hospital
I saw a specialist who told me they could do
nothing more for me. Twice before I had been
hospitalized for this same infection, and both
times I had checked myself out of the hospital
in faith, believing God would heal me. Instead
the infection got worse. This was my third

hospitalization. Now I did not seem to have much time left.

At the end of this third hospital stay I felt as if God was saying I needed to go to Toronto. I checked out of the hospital, knowing my destiny was to live and not die because of all the promises God had already given me.

Sometimes when God wants to heal you, He may ask you to get up, go somewhere, or do something. You may need to do more than sit there, hoping for someone to touch you. If you have arthritis, He might say, "Get up and dance." If you have depression, He might say, "Rejoice!" It need not make sense to anyone else.

I said to Rolland, "We need to get on a plane right now and go to Toronto because God told me to." I was scheduled to speak at a church there. They did not really expect me to come because they knew I was sick, though at the time they did not know how severe my illness really was.

I arrived in Toronto pale as a ghost and extremely weak. I would have fallen over if someone had touched me. I had my running shoes packed in my suitcase though.

When they saw me, the leaders there were

scared. They had a doctor there who wanted to hook me up with an IV immediately. They assured me I did not have to speak. I told them I had come a long way and that I was most definitely going to preach that night.

They were extremely nervous, but they let me have my way. I asked their doctor to lay his hands on me and pray instead of putting in an IV. Then, slowly, I managed to make my way up to the stage. God told me that I was to release the word from Zechariah. I made it to the pulpit, holding on to it for dear life so I would not fall down. I began by quoting Zechariah 2:5 (NIV): "'I myself will be a wall of fire around it,' declares the LORD, 'and I will be its glory within.'"

As I read the verse, all at once the glory of the Lord hit me. It felt like electricity going up and down my body. A torrent of God's fire went from my head to my toes three times. I was totally, completely, instantly healed. All the weakness and pain left my body. The sores completely closed up. One moment with King Jesus and all was well.

I was transformed right there in front of those people. They did not know the full significance of what had happened, but I knew and God knew. The next day I put on my running shoes and jogged! It was a truly miraculous healing.

Thought for Reflection

What does it mean to you to "hope against hope"? Are you "fully persuaded" that God is able to do what He has promised to do in your life?

Prayer

Lord, work miracles in and through me. Though there may be rough times ahead, I believe that You will fulfill Your word to me. Help me to obey You even when what You ask of me doesn't make sense to my natural mind.

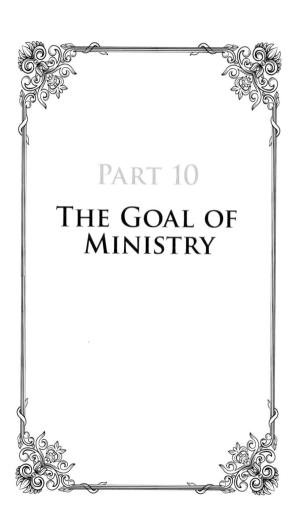

PART 10

THE GOAL OF
MINISTRY

DAY 90
RELEASING
SUPERNATURAL LOVE

*I heard the voice of the Lord saying, "Whom
shall I send, and who will go for us?" Then
I said, "Here am I. Send me."*
—ISAIAH 6:8

I had a vision several years after coming to Mozambique in which the Lord showed me how He was going to release a movement of supernatural love across the face of the earth. In this vision I was taken up to heaven and suspended above the earth. Around the earth, surrounding the entire globe, I saw thousands upon thousands of chariots of fire. They were carrying the glory of the Lord.

Inside each chariot sat two saints of God. They were totally transparent; there was nothing hidden in them. There was no darkness, nothing disguised, nothing covering them. They were transparent and full of glory, full of light.

There was only one spot of color inside each saint. It was a huge, immense heart that went shoulder to shoulder. It was a heart beating with love and passion. It was a huge, red heart.

I looked up to heaven, and there was Jesus. He is so beautiful! His eyes of love were looking upon me, melting me, causing my heart to go bigger still.

I saw His heart, and it was beating. I saw it beating, and I heard it beating. I looked in the chariots at the saints of God, and each huge heart of love was beating in rhythm with the heartbeat of Jesus.

Each saint held a gleaming white-gold sword, and flames of fire were coming off it. It took two hands—two holy hands—to hold each sword.

Two white magnificent horses led each chariot. They were ready to run! They had veins on their necks and bits in their mouths. The reins were reaching straight up to heaven.

The Lord Jesus said to me, "Tell the church, 'Release control.' I will hold the reins to this revival. I will decide where the chariots run.

Tell the church to release the reins to Me. Holy is the Lamb."

And then I saw the Lord's right hand straight above His head, and He cried, "Now!" As His right hand went down, the chariots of fire and glory began to run across the face of the earth.

As the chariots ran across the earth, glory fire fell upon the earth. Glory fire began to burn upon the earth, and the earth was ablaze.

But there were pockets on the earth that resisted the glory, the mercy, and even the love of Jesus. Those pockets upon the earth became hideous darkness like nothing I had ever seen. There were holes of hideous darkness like something I could never have imagined.

I looked at my Jesus, and He said, "The sword is both mercy and judgment. For those who will receive My love, there is great mercy, compassion, kindness, and glory, but for those who will reject My presence, My purpose, My love, there is great darkness and judgment."

I saw the gray that was upon the earth disappear. There was only darkness and light—and the light increased until the earth became ablaze with fire wherever the chariots ran. Where the transparent saints with huge hearts of love ran across the earth, there was great light, for the love of Jesus conquered the darkness through them.

The Lord asked me to ask the church: "Who will ride in the chariots of glory, carrying the huge heart of Jesus's love within them? Who will ride in the chariots of glory and not touch or steal the glory? Who will take the holy sword of the Lord in their hands? Who will release control to the Bridegroom King?"

Thought for Reflection

The Lord is asking who will go, who will carry His love and light throughout the earth. Will you?

Prayer

Lord, You are working miracles around the world. Supernatural things are happening, and I want to be involved in them. Let me be one who goes. Help me to carry Your love and spread it to the lost, poor, and broken.

DAY 91
FALL IN LOVE WITH JESUS

*"Teacher, which is the greatest commandment
in the law?" Jesus said to him, "'You shall love
the Lord your God with all your heart, and
with all your soul, and with all your mind.'
This is the first and great commandment."*
—MATTHEW 22:36–38

Union and communion with God: this is
the essence of Christianity. We must give up
all that we are in order to possess all that He
is. We must yield who we are to become one
with Him. The foundation of your calling
is intimacy with Him. If you are not in love
with Jesus, I loudly cry, "Quit!," until you find
His love so that you can carry it to others.

Don't go out to share Him unless you are
in love with Him. When you are in love with
Jesus, then all you do will radiate Him.

It is to the degree that you are in love that
you radiate Him. If you are not in love enough,

then you need more time with Him. My life is busy. But the busier I get, the more time I need with Jesus. When I minister, I must minister out of the fullness of my unity with Him. Our first pleasure is to be united with Jesus—to be one with the man Christ Jesus.

Our greatest joy in life is to be married to Jesus so that we can give our lives away without fear, just as He did for us. My goal is that you fall so deeply in love with Him that there is not a "no" left in you when responding to the high calling of God in Christ Jesus. When you are full of the presence of God and another person meets you, it is the same as that person's meeting Him. Jesus becomes irresistible to him. When you hold him, Jesus holds him.

Missions and ministry are simply about laid-down lovers at the foot of the cross, praying, "Possess me, Holy Spirit, that I might be conformed into the image of Jesus. Let me reflect the majesty of who He is." Let Jesus love you first so that you can love others as He did. When you lose yourself inside His huge heart, you find only pure joy in Him.

Thought for Reflection

Your first responsibility in this life is to seek union and communion with the Lord. It is from this that all ministry flows. Can you claim today that you are truly in love with Him?

Prayer

Lord, please meet with me and set my heart on fire with love for You. I want to know You intimately. I want people who meet me to see You.

DAY 92
LOVE IS THE GOAL

If I speak with the tongues of men and of angels, and have not love, I have become as sounding brass or a clanging cymbal. If I have the gift of prophecy, and understand all mysteries and all knowledge, and if I have all faith, so that I could remove mountains, and have not love, I am nothing. If I give all my goods to feed the poor, and if I give my body to be burned, and have not love, it profits me nothing.
—1 CORINTHIANS 13:1–3

Like Jesus, we have only one aim and goal: to love. Our mission is passion and compassion; we are to love God and to love our neighbor, as Jesus tells us in the two greatest commandments. (See Matthew 22:36–40.)

All that Jesus did flowed from that abandoned place of laid-down love. With *compassion* He embraced the man with leprosy, held the dying woman, broke the law to sit at the well, and talked to the prostitute. "But when

He saw the crowds, He was moved with compassion for them, because they fainted and were scattered, like sheep without a shepherd. Then He said to His disciples, 'The harvest truly is plentiful, but the laborers are few. Therefore, pray to the Lord of the harvest, that He will send out laborers into His harvest'" (Matt. 9:37–38).

Ministry is being one of these sent-out ones—a laborer of love. If ministry is not about compassion and passion, let it die.

Ministry is all about love. In Philippians 2, Paul—who was, after Jesus, one of the greatest sent-out ones to walk the planet—writes: "If there is any encouragement in Christ, if any comfort of love, if any fellowship of the Spirit, if any compassion and mercy, then fulfill my joy and be like-minded, having the same love, being in unity with one mind" (vv. 1–2). Paul exhorts us to have the same kind of heart, motivation, and love as Christ Jesus. Love is tender. Love is filled with compassion. This exhortation lived out would change the very face of Christianity.

Jesus is the ultimate example of God's dwelling among us. Love Himself walked the earth. We fix our gaze on Jesus as the perfect model of life. Before Jesus spoke about love in the Sermon on the Mount, He demonstrated it. He healed diseases and helped those suffering from severe pain and demon possession. He preached the gospel.

God has called us to this simplicity of love. I do not feel called to what many call greatness or success. My only call is to love more.

Thought for Reflection

In your ministry is love your primary goal? You can work and serve endlessly, but if you don't love those you serve, your work is meaningless. God has called His bride to love without limits.

Prayer

Lord, the gospel message really is simple: it is to love as You love. Thank You for giving me Your love and allowing me to share it with others.

Day 93
Learning to Love

Let all that you do be done with love.
—1 CORINTHIANS 16:14

I believe that when we die and go to heaven, God will have only one question for us: Did you learn to love? He expects the same from us as He did from His Son. Love in action is what moves His heart, as Mother Teresa points out:

> Love has no meaning if it isn't shared. Love has to be put into action. You have to love without expectation, do something for love itself, not for what you may receive.[1]

> Love in action is what gives us grace. We have been created for greater things...to love and to be loved. Love is love—to love a person without any conditions, without any expectations.

> Small things, done in great love,
> bring joy and peace. To love, it is nec-
> essary to give. To give, it is necessary
> to be free from selfishness.[2]

We are created to bring the love of Jesus—love without limits—to those who are in need. God does not say the poor will always be good, kind, or thankful; yet He calls us to always love them.

Love will cost you everything: laying down your life, living a life of passion and compassion, giving without expecting, feeling God's very heartbeat, surrendering to His rhythm, and following the Lamb wherever He goes—even to the ends of the earth.

Why go to the ends of the earth if you have nothing to give? The only currency that will heal every culture is ceaseless love. To be a minister, you must walk like Jesus, talk like Jesus, and be like Jesus for a broken and dying world.

Ministry looks like servanthood manifested through love. Your job description is to be the fragrance of Christ, the beauty of Jesus, and the very anointing of Him on the earth. As you minister, you minister in

Him. As you walk, you walk in Him. Jesus told the Father: "I do not pray for these [His disciples] alone, but also for those who will believe in Me through their word, that they may all be one, as You, Father, are in Me, and I in You. May they also be one in Us, that the world may believe that You have sent Me. I have given them the glory which You gave Me, that they may be one even as We are one: I in them and You in Me, that they may be perfect in unity, and that the world may know that You have sent Me, and have loved them as You have loved Me" (John 17:20–23).

Thought for Reflection

Learning how to love is essential to fulfilling the call of God on your life. Do you feel as if you are growing in this area? Are you able to love as Jesus loved? Commit today to letting every action you take be done in love.

Prayer

Lord, I know that I can spend the rest of my life learning to love as You love. Teach me, and use me to show love to others, even while I'm still learning.

DAY 94
LOVE WITHOUT LIMIT

You have heard that it was said, "You shall love your neighbor and hate your enemy." But I say to you, love your enemies, bless those who curse you, do good to those who hate you, and pray for those who spitefully use you and persecute you, that you may be sons of your Father who is in heaven."
—MATTHEW 5:43–45

It's easy to love those around you when they are your family and friends. It is more difficult to love those who hate you and who harm you or the people close to you. Yet God calls us to love others as He does—unconditionally—regardless of who they are or how they treat us.

I have learned this lesson more than once. But this time I felt angry. I did not understand why God would give us so many children and then allow them to be beaten and made homeless. I knew theologically that

Father God loved us and loved the children, but I did not understand how to be a peacemaker in the situation we were facing.

I remember looking into the faces of the children one by one, trying to think what would bring them hope. Since the first day I had picked them up from the streets, I had taught the children, "We must love without limit. We will love without end."

A friend of mine, who had been a soldier during the war, was very protective of me. One day, when a twenty-dollar contract was put out on my life, he came to me and said, "Don't worry, Mama Aida. I have a plan!" He promised to protect me. He told me he had an AK-47 and a grenade under his bed. He said, "I will go and kill them for you."

He thought I would be very happy to hear of his offer to me, but I turned to him and said, "We are here to love and to bring peace."

I made a decision to go back to the center in broad daylight. I knew about the danger to my life, but I wanted to speak to my village friends about love and forgiveness. I shared my heart with them and told them,

"I want you to love those who want to kill us. I want you to love them without limit and without end. I want you to make peace with them."

We could have left and gone to America to escape all the craziness. We could have gone to the international press and fought our case, but we kept hearing the Lord call us to love and forgive.

My message will never change. All I have to give is love. Daily I ask Jesus for more courage to love without limit.

Thought for Reflection

Who in your life is difficult to love? Who would you consider an enemy? Are you willing to extend God's love to them and to bless them, do good to them, and pray for them as Jesus commands? What will that look like?

Prayer

Lord, the bottom line is love—Your love expressed through me to others. That is all You require. You loved me with a powerful and mighty love that changed my whole life; now it's my turn to love those around me with that kind of love. Give me the grace and strength to do so even when it is not easy.

DAY 95
FULFILLING GOD'S CALL
REQUIRES SACRIFICE

*According to His custom, He came out and went
to the Mount of Olives. And His disciples followed Him. When He came there, He said to
them, "Pray that you may not fall into temptation." He withdrew from them about a stone's
throw, and He knelt down and prayed, "Father, if
You are willing, remove this cup from Me. Nevertheless not My will, but Yours, be done."*
—LUKE 22:39–42

As believers we all have a mighty calling to
carry God's heart and to reveal His glorious
love to the world. None of us can fully imagine or expect what the Lord has for us or what
the journey to the fulfillment of His promises
will look like. I don't think Mary was expecting to carry a child before she was married or
to give birth to the Son of God. She could
never have anticipated the magnitude of the

call or the price she would have to pay. But because our lives are not our own, we must be willing to say yes to the call no matter what God requires of us. Jesus, who submitted to God's will after receiving a "no" when He asked God to change it, is our example.

One day I was at a church conference in the Middle East when I found myself listening to a speaker who didn't know I was present. Evidently he had no idea I was scheduled to speak right after him. Since I was preparing to minister, I was surprised and dismayed when I realized he was talking negatively about my life and ministry.

I wanted to hide. I wanted to run away and never speak there again. But first I prayed, and I felt the Holy Spirit reminding me that my life is not my own. I believed God had asked me to share in this place, so I obeyed. When I walked out on that stage, it felt as if I was dying again. Mercifully the Lord came and touched people with power. I became very aware, yet again, that my life is not my own. We are in His hands, and He uses us as He desires.

We are paintbrushes in the hands of the

Master. We cannot paint, but He can. I always say to God that if He can use a donkey, He can use me. He could use a rock if He wanted to. If we understand the cross, we know our lives are not our own; they belong to Him. We have been bought with a price. With that in mind, what then will we live for?

I don't think any great thing we are called to do has only natural consequences. Rather, the precious fruit of eternal significance comes when God's heart is manifested in and through us. As we walk obediently in the paths He sets for us, He reveals more details about what we've been created to do and how we are to do it. I believe the Lord, in His kindness, reveals our destiny to us in stages. He shows us His dream and His desire for the world.

There is a daily sacrifice and a daily joy as we participate in God's dreams for this world, as we let Him use and shape us. As we do this, we participate with Jesus in the sacrifices He too made for the joy that was set before Him. What an awesome privilege!

Thought for Reflection

The Lord wants to use you, but it may not always be easy for you to answer His call. You may have days on which difficult things are asked of you. Don't pull back in these times; give God a chance to paint His masterpiece through you.

Prayer

Lord, use me. Use me even in difficult situations I would rather not be in. Help me to get out of the way so You can move. Let me be a simple paintbrush in Your hands.

DAY 96
DISCERN WHAT IS BEST

*This I pray, that your love may abound yet more
and more in knowledge and in all discernment.*
—PHILIPPIANS 1:9

Once when I asked the Lord for a message to share with our Iris family, He led me to Philippians. Paul's prayer for the body of Christ was "that your love may abound yet more and more in knowledge and in all discernment, that you may approve things that are excellent so that you may be pure and blameless for the day of Christ, being filled with the fruit of righteousness, which comes through Jesus Christ, for the glory and praise of God" (Phil. 1:9–11).

How do we discern what is best? God tells us in the secret place. Beloved, Jesus never makes us tired. He never burns us out. He longs for us to burn continuously with fiery passion and love for Him and for the lost.

If you feel tired and burned out, run to the secret place. Even if you feel joyful and ready to take on whatever may come, don't forget to dwell in the secret place and receive Daddy God's plans for each day.

God also gave me a prophetic picture. I saw a chicken and an eagle. The chicken was running around in circles in the dirt. He flapped and flapped and ran in circles to no avail. A chicken simply cannot fly. The strangest thing about chickens is that even if their heads are cut off, they don't know they're dead. They just keep flapping and running in circles. Sometimes we can get so caught up in the needs around us that we don't even notice we are dead and have been separated from our head, Christ Jesus.

In the prophetic picture I also saw an eagle. An eagle soars! He barely needs to flap his wings because he is carried on the wind and sees with heavenly perspective. Our service to God can be the same way. As Isaiah 40:31 says, "Those who hope in the LORD will renew their strength. They will soar on wings like eagles; they will run and not grow weary, they will walk and not be faint" (NIV).

Thought for Reflection

I'm sure you've heard the saying, "Don't run around like a chicken with its head cut off." What does it mean to you with regard to your spiritual life? How can you be less like a chicken and more like an eagle when it comes to serving God? The devotion offers one answer: spend time in the secret place so that you can learn from God what is best and avoid getting tired and burned out. Allow Him to renew your strength and cause you to "soar on wings like eagles" (Isa. 40:31, NIV).

Prayer

Lord, help me not to grow weary in well-doing. Teach me how to be renewed in Your presence so that I can soar like an eagle, being carried by the wind of the Spirit, rather than striving to serve You out of my own effort.

DAY 97
WORKING TOGETHER
FOR THE HARVEST

For by one Spirit we are all baptized into one body,
whether we are Jews or Gentiles, whether we are
slaves or free, and we have all been made to drink of
one Spirit. The body is not one part, but many....If
the whole body were hearing, where would the sense
of smell be? But now God has established the parts,
every one of them, in the body as it has pleased
Him....So there are many parts, yet one body.
—1 CORINTHIANS 12:13–14, 17–18, 20

If you have ever taken a look inside an art-
ist's paint box, you will see many different
sizes and shapes of paintbrushes. Each brush
is designed for a particular function. The art-
ist would never be able to create a masterpiece
with only one type of brush. He chooses each
one carefully depending on what he desires
to put on his canvas.

Similarly God wants to work through each

of us using the personalities and gifts unique to us, and He expresses His love through each of us in a unique way. After all, original works of art are far more valuable than copies. Even though we are only little paintbrushes or little pots, we are made individually, and no one else is like us. The Holy Spirit flows through each vessel, revealing God's dream for the world and our own place within it. What a glorious plan!

Even so, we cannot do the work of God all on our own. We need the hands and feet and hearts and minds of other people, all working together to bring God's great kingdom to fruition on the earth. We need each other.

I began to see this in even greater measure one day when I was praying with friends in Mozambique. During our time of prayer I saw a vision of a huge fishing net being let down from heaven. When I saw the net, I was thrilled because I thought it was a net for Iris Global, representing all the great work we would do and the growth we would see.

I felt as if the Lord chuckled and showed me that Iris Global was just a little piece of that vast net. He showed me some of the other pieces. I saw the Assemblies of God, the International House of Prayer, Bethel Church, the Toronto church, the Baptists, Youth With A Mission, the Nazarenes, Operation Blessing, World Vision, and many other movements across the earth. They were each serving and loving Him. I felt the Lord say that only when we work together will we bring in the harvest.

Thought for Reflection

We are not called to be "lone rangers," extending the kingdom of God on our own. We must seek to be faithful to do what we are called to accomplish and to trust God to bring others alongside us who have the personalities and gifts to do what we cannot.

Prayer

Lord, thank You for making me unique and for helping me to use my gifts and talents as You intended. Thank You also for calling other members of the body to accomplish different tasks for Your kingdom so that together we may bring in the harvest and give You glory.

DAY 98
NOW IS THE TIME
FOR GOD'S PROMISE

Look, now is the accepted time; look,
now is the day of salvation.
—2 CORINTHIANS 6:2

Sometimes it seems as if time is running
out for God to fulfill His promises to us. Yet
we know that He doesn't require a particular
number of days, months, or years to bring
them to fruition. He can work in an instant
when it suits Him.

The Lord spoke to me about His timing
through the birth of one of my grandbabies
in Mozambique. One of my adopted sons,
Jacinto, and his wife, Katie, were about to
have their second child. I was very excited
about this birth. I had also been present at
the birth of their first son, Micah. There
was only one problem: Katie went into labor
just before I was scheduled to fly out of the

country on a speaking tour. Their first baby had taken thirty hours to be born. I could not wait that long. And Katie certainly did not want another lengthy labor!

When I got to the house, Katie was only one centimeter dilated. I watched this beautiful spiritual daughter of mine screaming in pain, and at that moment I wanted nothing more than for it to stop. I held her hand and began to walk with her while praying in the Spirit.

Suddenly a strong prophetic urge came over me. The Lord stirred my heart, and I began to declare that she would go from one centimeter dilated to ten—*now*. I believe that as I spoke the word over Katie, and other intercessors were also praying, an amazing miracle happened.

Suddenly Katie went into full labor. Her baby came supernaturally quickly. It had been only forty-five minutes since the strong contractions began when she gave birth to a beautiful baby boy. It might have been the easiest birth I have ever seen.

I lifted up my grandchild to Jesus, and I dedicated him to Father God. Then I handed him to Jacinto and left for the airport. I got on the plane just in time.

When we go through painful seasons and trials in our lives, we do not want our suffering to be prolonged. I believe Katie's child was released supernaturally quickly as a prophetic sign for the times. Many of you have been given prophetic words and promises that would seem to require long and difficult transitions before they could ever come to pass. You may have begun to feel that these promises are never going to come true because there is not enough time left for you to see them fulfilled. I believe this word is for you and that now is the time for God's promise to be supernaturally birthed in your life.

Thought for Reflection

It is time for God's promises to be birthed in our lives. A natural birth is often long and painful, but God is eager to perform miracles of supernatural swiftness on behalf of His children. Are you ready?

Prayer

Lord, I believe the time is now for me to see Your promise fulfilled in my life. I pray that You prepare me to receive it and act on it.

Day 99
The Fruit of Obedience

Therefore, my beloved brothers, be steadfast, unmovable, always abounding in the work of the Lord, knowing that your labor in the Lord is not in vain.
—1 CORINTHIANS 15:58

As Rolland and I reflect back over the years, it is clear we never anticipated how high the cost of our calling would be. Likewise, I think Mary could not have known the extent of the pain she would have to go through—including watching her own Son crucified. You will likely be called to pay a higher price than you have ever imagined as well.

But we also never anticipated the unceasing joy. We have witnessed incredibly abundant fruit, both in our lives and in the lives of those walking alongside us in this beautiful movement that has flowered so far beyond our dreams.

We continually hear stories of people so

touched by the Lord that they feel compelled to yield up their whole lives in return. We rejoice in them all. It is our privilege to see so many saying yes to the joy and the cost of life in the secret place. More than anything we want to see a multiplication of His manifest love in the world.

We are building a university to train Mozambican leaders to transform their nation. This property involves a decade-long journey. The Lord spoke to me to build a university while I was snorkeling one day. I was in total shock and sucked water into my throat!

Then the Lord spoke to me about the time He healed me from severe dyslexia when I was sixteen years old and a baby Christian. My high school teachers told me I would never go to university and should simply pursue vocational training, but God called me to complete my bachelor's degree. Many times I wanted to drop out and move to Africa; I kept thinking about my calling and the lost. But every time the Lord spoke to me to continue my studies, and I obeyed.

In my early twenties, while serving as a missionary in Asia, I heard the Lord clearly say that by the time I was twenty-five I would have my master's degree. Earning it meant leaving Hong Kong and all the people I loved for a season of more preparation.

A few years later while serving in Hong Kong again, I got extraordinarily sick with an immune system disorder and was not able to read or concentrate. As I was praying in this seriously sick condition, the Lord spoke to me that it was time to go and earn my PhD! I was in shock once again. How could I earn a PhD when I was in such terrible health? How could I leave Asia where there was so much fruit? I knew in the end I would simply obey. I felt called to go to King's College at the University of London and study systematic theology. Four years later I defended my thesis with an external examiner and graduated.

The point is, if I hadn't obeyed the Lord when I was sixteen, I would not have been able to receive my next promise. Now, as we build the university, I clearly see why God led me to get my PhD. Sometimes we do not understand the direction He takes us in, but He is always trustworthy and always faithful.

What incredible fruit awaits us on the other side of our obedience!

Thought for Reflection

Are you slow to obey God when what He is asking will require you to pay a high price? At these times think of the fruit you will bear. Remember the joy you will experience, and say yes without hesitation.

Prayer

Lord, I know that not everything You ask me to do will be easy. Give me the grace to obey nevertheless, and help me to find joy in witnessing the fruit that is borne.

DAY 100
BUILDING A LEGACY

*Share the things that you have heard from me
in the presence of many witnesses with faithful men who will be able to teach others also.*
—2 TIMOTHY 2:2

Whether you are just beginning to fulfill
God's call on your life or have been engaging
in it for a long time, it is important to
consider how God may want to extend your
reach through others that He asks you to
train. There is no need to wait until you are
old; begin mentoring now so that you will
leave a legacy for those who come after you.

Through the years God has allowed me
to pour my life into many people. I have
had the privilege of imparting His heart
for children and the poor around the world.
When God ignites people's hearts in this
way, they begin to rescue children. They feed
them, house them, and educate them. The

ones they care for are part of my vision for a million children. Ministers who have spent time at Iris and then left to begin their own organizations are also a part of it. The vision is not only for Rolland and me; it belongs to many faithful men and women around the world. It is a legacy for our children and our children's children.

Rolland and I believe we are called to cheer on the next generation of laid-down lovers. As they run into the darkness to love the broken and bring the lost children home, we want our ceiling to be their floor.

There is a price to raising up the next generation, but when we see them thrive, that cost seems like nothing. When a mother goes into labor, there is excruciating pain, pushing, and transition. There is incredible stretching. Blood vessels burst.

When I held my first baby and looked into his eyes, I completely forgot about the pain of childbirth. When we were ready to have another child, there was not a single moment when the prospect of pain made me think I could not do it again. When the time came, I held my daughter in my arms and felt the same awesome love. The joy of bearing a child is greater than the cost of suffering.

It is the same with spiritual things. When you see your sons and daughters raised up and saying yes to the destiny God extends to them, you feel blessed and privileged that you were able to pay a price to help them.

As we have been getting older, we have been thinking a lot about legacy. Recently the Lord has put it on our hearts that we must seek to grow and support not only Iris Global but also a far wider move of God that encompasses hundreds and thousands of men, women, and children who are venturing fearlessly into the darkness of the earth for the sake of the gospel.

What about you? What legacy does God want you to start building now?

Thought for Reflection

You have promises from God and a calling on your life to fulfill, but part of your work should include building a legacy for others to carry on. Ask God for discernment to help you recognize those you should invest in—the ones

who will take up the vision He has put
on your heart.

Prayer

*Lord, prepare me to build a legacy of laid-
down lovers. Make me willing to train
others, and give me the discernment to
know when it is time to take a step back
and allow others to step up.*

NOTES

Day 16
Pure in Heart

1. Mother Teresa, *In My Own Words*, comp.
   José Luis González-Balado (New York:
   Gramercy Books, a division of Random
   House Value Publishing, Inc., 1996).

Day 28
Eat and Drink of Me

1. Mother Teresa, *No Greater Love*, ed. Becky
   Benenate and Joseph Durepos, rev. ed.
   (Novato, CA: New World Library, 1997).
   Originally published as *The Mother Teresa
   Reader: A Life for God*, comp. LaVonne Neff,
   rev. ed. (Ann Arbor, MI: Servant Publica-
   tions, Inc., 1995).

Day 58
We Need One Another

1. Mother Teresa, *In My Own Words*.

Day 59
Childlike Faith

1. Mother Teresa, *No Greater Love*.

Day 71
Holy Desperation

1. Mother Teresa, *No Greater Love*.

Day 93
Learning to Love

1. Mother Teresa, *One Heart Full of Love* (Ann Arbor, MI: Servant Publications, 1988), 87.
2. Mother Teresa, *No Greater Love*.

CONNECT WITH US!

CHARISMA HOUSE

(Spiritual Growth)

[f] Facebook.com/CharismaHouse

[🐦] @CharismaHouse

[📷] Instagram.com/CharismaHouseBooks

SILOAM

(Health)

[📌] Pinterest.com/CharismaHouse

REALMS

(Fiction)

[f] Facebook.com/RealmsFiction